T0318171

Human Development and the Catholic Social Tradition

This book brings development theory and practice into dialogue with a religious tradition in order to construct a new, transdisciplinary vision of development with integral ecology at its heart.

It focuses on the Catholic social tradition and its conception of integral human development, on the one hand, and on the works of economist and philosopher Amartya Sen which underpin the human development approach, on the other. The book discusses how these two perspectives can mutually enrich each other around three areas: their views on the concept and meaning of development and progress; their understanding of what it is to be human – that is, their anthropological vision; and their analysis of transformational pathways for addressing social and environmental degradation. It also examines how both human development and the Catholic social tradition can function as complementary analytical lenses and mobilizing frames for embarking on the journey of structural and personal transformation to bring all life systems, human and non-human, back into balance.

This book is written for researchers and students in development studies, theology, and religious studies, as well as professional audiences in development organizations.

Séverine Deneulin is Director of International Development at the Laudato Si' Research Institute, Campion Hall, University of Oxford, UK; and Associate Professor of International Development at the University of Bath, UK.

Routledge Research in Religion and Development
Series Editors:
Matthew Clarke, *Deakin University, Australia*
Emma Tomalin, *University of Leeds, UK*
Nathan Loewen, *University of Alabama, USA*
Editorial board:
Carole Rakodi, *University of Birmingham, UK*
Gurharpal Singh, *School of Oriental and African Studies, University of London, UK*
Jörg Haustein, *School of Oriental and African Studies, University of London, UK*
Christopher Duncanson-Hales, *Saint Paul University, Canada*

The Routledge Research in Religion and Development series focuses on the diverse ways in which religious values, teachings and practices interact with international development.

While religious traditions and faith-based movements have long served as forces for social innovation, it has only been within the last ten years that researchers have begun to seriously explore the religious dimensions of international development. However, recognising and analysing the role of religion in the development domain is vital for a nuanced understanding of this field. This interdisciplinary series examines the intersection between these two areas, focusing on a range of contexts and religious traditions.

Adapting Gender and Development to Local Religious Contexts
A Decolonial Approach to Domestic Violence in Ethiopia
Romina Istratii

Human Development and the Catholic Social Tradition
Towards an Integral Ecology
Séverine Deneulin

For more information about this series, please visit: www.routledge.com/Routledge-Research-in-Religion-and-Development/book-series/RRRD

Human Development and the Catholic Social Tradition

Towards an Integral Ecology

Séverine Deneulin

Routledge
Taylor & Francis Group
LONDON AND NEW YORK

First published 2021
by Routledge
2 Park Square, Milton Park, Abingdon, Oxon OX14 4RN

and by Routledge
605 Third Avenue, New York, NY 10017

Routledge is an imprint of the Taylor & Francis Group, an informa business

British Library Cataloguing-in-Publication Data
A catalogue record for this book is available from the British Library

Library of Congress Cataloging-in-Publication Data
Names: Deneulin, Séverine, 1974– author.
Title: Human development and the Catholic social tradition : towards an integral ecology / Séverine Deneulin.
Description: Abingdon, Oxon ; New York, NY : Routledge, [2022] | Series: Routledge research in religion and development | Includes bibliographical references and index.
Identifiers: LCCN 2021006637 (print) | LCCN 2021006638 (ebook)
Subjects: LCSH: Christian sociology—Catholic Church. | Sen, Amartya, 1933– | Catholic Church—Doctrines. | Encyclicals, Papal—History and criticism. | Social participation. | Human ecology—Religious aspects—Catholic Church.
Classification: LCC BX1753 .D39 2022 (print) | LCC BX1753 (ebook) | DDC 261/.1—dc23
LC record available at https://lccn.loc.gov/2021006637
LC ebook record available at https://lccn.loc.gov/2021006638

ISBN 13: 978-0-367-63961-7 (hbk)
ISBN 13: 978-0-367-63963-1 (pbk)

DOI: 10.4324/9781003121534

Contents

Acknowledgements

This book was written between August 2020 and January 2021, but the process of thinking about it started many years earlier, and a large number of people have helped me in this process. I first presented a paper on Amartya Sen's capability approach in dialogue with the Catholic tradition at the fortieth anniversary conference of the Second Vatican Council document *Gaudium et Spes* (*Joy and Hope*) in Rome in April 2005. I had just finished a DPhil in development studies on Amartya Sen, and someone invited to the conference insisted I should attend too. I thought I had nothing to contribute, but, with his insistence, set myself the task of engaging Amartya Sen's thought with the theology of the Second Vatican Council. The participants' encouragement proved to be a turning point. One of the conference organizers, Johan Verstraeten, has continued to be a strong support since then.

Shortly after the conference, Susy Brouard, then at the Catholic Agency for Overseas Development (CAFOD), invited me to write a reflection on Pope Paul VI's encyclical *Populorum Progressio* (PP, *On the Progress of Peoples*) and the UNDP *Human Development Reports*. I renewed work on the dialogue between Amartya Sen and the Catholic social tradition a few years afterwards when Augusto Zampini-Davies did a master's dissertation on the topic at the University of Bath, and then a PhD. Consequently, we organized several workshops with social scientists, theologians, and development practitioners bringing the two into conversation. The discussions at these workshops underpin a lot of this book's arguments.

It took several years to bring the idea of a monograph on the subject to fruition. I thank especially Celia Deane-Drummond and the intellectual space of the Laudato Si' Research Institute at Campion Hall, Oxford, for giving me the impetus and motivation finally to write a book. I also thank Helena Hurd at Routledge for her support of the project and three anonymous referees for their comments on the proposal. Nick Townsend witnessed my return to London from the 2005 conference in Rome and has been an intellectual companion in working to develop the Catholic social tradition ever since. I am immensely grateful for his careful reading of the manuscript, and his incisive comments, corrections, and edits. Any error (or long, French-style sentences!) remains mine.

Abbreviations

CA – *Centesimus Annus*: On the Hundreth Anniversary of Rerum Novarum (Pope John Paul II, 1st May 1991)

CV – Caritas in Veritate: Charity in Truth (Pope Benedict XVI, 29th June 2009)

EG – *Evangelii Gaudium*: The Joy of the Gospel (Pope Francis, 24th November 2013)

FT – Fratelli Tutti: On Fraternity and Social Friendship (Pope Francis, 3rd October 2020)

LS – Laudato Si': On Care for our Common Home (Pope Francis, 24th May 2015)

PP – Populorum Progressio: On the Progress of Peoples (Pope Paul VI, 26th March 1967)

QA – Querida Amazonia: Beloved Amazon (Pope Francis, 2nd February 2020)

RN – Rerum Novarum: On New Things (Pope Leon XIII, 15th May 1891)

SRS – Sollicitudo Rei Socialis: On Social Concerns (John Paul II, 30th December 1987)

These documents will be referred throughout the text by the initial of the first two letters of their title, followed by the corresponding paragraph.

Introduction

It is now two decades since religion entered development studies as a research subject. The World Bank study *Voices of the Poor* (Narayan et al. 2000) was a turning point in the relationship between development organizations and faith communities, and between development research and religion. The study gathered the voices of more than 60,000 people across more than 40 countries on how they understood what it meant to live well and on their experience of being poor. Among the findings from this extensive participatory exercise were the observations that, for many people, religion permeated people's conception of living well, that sacred places held an important place in people's lives (Narayan et al. 2000: 38, 234), and that religious institutions were often more trusted than state institutions – though they did not excel in accountability and participatory decision-making (Narayan et al. 2000: 179). From something deemed private with no public or development implications, or something deemed superstition which would disappear as people became more educated, religion became something that had to be reckoned with for anyone or any organization concerned with reducing poverty and improving people's lives. Not least, the World Bank study brought to the fore the reality that religious organizations, known in the literature as faith-based organizations, were significant providers of social services – such as health and education – among the poorest communities worldwide, leading to a new interest in faith-based organizations as key development actors.[1]

The adoption of Agenda 2030 for Sustainable Development and their 17 Sustainable Development Goals (SDGs) at the United Nations (UN) General Assembly in September 2015 as a 'shared blueprint for peace and prosperity for people and the planet'[2] led to further interest in the role of religion and faith-based actors in development (Tomalin et al. 2019).[3] An international partnership for religion and development was formed to bring governmental and intergovernmental entities together with civil society and faith communities to promote the SDGs.[4] However, in the midst of this

DOI: 10.4324/9781003121534-1

greater rapprochement and collaboration, concerns have also been raised about the dangers of instrumentalizing faith communities for the sake of an externally imposed agenda (Petersen and Jones 2011; Tomalin 2020) and about the lack of interest in how faith communities themselves conceive of the SDGs and how they translate and transform them within their own frames. While people within one perspective might speak of 'protecting life below water' and 'protecting life on land' (cf. SDG 14 and 15), those with a different one might speak of 'protecting all of God's creation'; and while one might say 'no poverty' and 'zero hunger' (SDG 1 and 2), the other might say 'attend to your sister and brother in need'.

The SDGs have been the subject of criticism for focusing too much on measurable results and not enough on processes and structural causes of climate change and poverty and inequality. They have also been criticized for glossing over conflicting, or incompatible, goals, such as SDG 8 on economic growth vis-à-vis the climate change–related goals (SDGs 12–15).[5] As much as faith actors have embraced the SDGs as part of a shared journey towards improving people's lives and addressing climate change, they are also urging policymakers and development practitioners 'to go beyond the SDG-agenda in order to redefine notions of growth, wealth and well-being' (Wuppertal Conference on Eco-Theology and the Ethics of Sustainability 2019: 12) and to start a genuine dialogue on the meanings and processes of global development and prosperity in an age of climate emergency.[6] The International Panel on Social Progress (IPSP 2018: 80–1) similarly urged for a genuine dialogue with religions, arguing that, because 'most spiritual belief systems address relationships between humans and the world around them, including non-human of all kinds', they have something to contribute to how we can reimagine how our societies can be organized and how they can be transformed.

At a time when a global zoonotic disease pandemic has revealed the human costs of the degradation of natural habitats,[7] and a global movement to 'build back better' is emerging,[8] this Routledge Research in Religion and Development Series Focus book examines what can be learned from faith communities about their own views on development and prosperity, what they see as desirable goals, and how these goals can be pursued. It also aims to bring the 'religion and development' research agenda to a new phase, beyond analysing religion and development as two independent variables which can form instrumental partnerships for achieving certain common goals, towards dialogue for mutual transformation. How could development theory and practice itself benefit from greater engagement with sources of wisdom coming from religious traditions? What can it learn from their perspectives on how we are to live, relate to others and to nature, and move into the future as a society? And could religious traditions themselves benefit from such engagement? These questions are at the core of this Routledge Focus book.

The notions of growth, wealth, prosperity, well-being, and 'change for the better'[9] have been at the core of development narratives since the first UN Development Decade in the 1960s. Since then, development has undergone a geographical transformation, from being about processes of change in developing countries – a broad term encompassing most ex-colonized countries but now categorizing different types of economies, social achievements, and state–society relations[10] – to being about addressing the problems of poverty and inequality globally (Horner and Hulme 2019). Development has unsurprisingly undergone many changes in meaning over the course of its history: from economic development; to social development; to sustainable development; to climate-compatible development (Nunan 2017); to abandoning the concept of development altogether (Rist 2014; Ziai 2017); to the SDGs; and to addressing the integrated challenges of poverty, inequality, and environmental degradation globally.[11] Development has also undergone a disciplinary transformation, from the dominance of economics and other social sciences to the greater inclusion of the natural sciences (Alff and Hornidge 2019). There is currently a move to decolonize development, to recognize the legitimacy and validity of different sources of knowledge (Schöneberg 2019), and to construct a 'new vision' for thinking about and doing development, which 'reflect[s] not only interdisciplinarity but also the trans-disciplinarity found in respect for multiple forms of knowledge' (Oswald, Leach and Gaventa 2019: 135).

This book aims at laying some building blocks for a transdisciplinary construction of a new vision of development by exploring the contributions of forms of knowledge coming from religious traditions to development studies. It explores how these two visions can mutually enrich each other and be combined to construct a new vision of development.

From within development studies, the vision selected as conversation partner is the one proposed by economist and philosopher Amartya Sen; it is known as the capability approach to development and has been translated as 'human development' by the United Nations Development Programme (UNDP) in its *Human Development Reports*.[12] Amartya Sen has, more than anyone in the field of development research, dealt with the fundamental normative questions of what constitutes development's ultimate ends and sought to shift the foundations of economics from utilitarian ethics to what some have called 'capabilitarian' ethics (Robeyns 2017). Sen's main critique of economics was that it reduced human well-being to considerations about utility, income, or subjective states of mind, and the human person to a rational self-interested maximizer (Sen 1977). His works have underlined the importance of value judgements for collective decision-making and policy. They have proposed a broader framework to that of utilitarianism for assessing whether one situation is better than another. For example, how to comparatively evaluate the merits of a city which has greater biodiversity and better air quality but lower income per capita, and a city with a higher income per capita but poorer air quality and biodiversity? Sen has argued for extending the information used to evaluate whether situation x is 'better' than situation y beyond information about utility or income or consumption to include considerations about what people are able to be and do, what he calls 'capabilities' (Sen 1993). His works have also sought to transform the reductive view of the human being as a utility maximizer to that of a person who exercises freedom and responsibility, for her life and that of others (Sen 1985).

As much as Amartya Sen has brought to the core of development studies the normative questions of how one should live, what constitutes 'better' social arrangements and outcomes, and how a society should move into the future, he has never proposed a specific moral standpoint from which to answer those questions. Even regarding the question of which criteria to use to assess whether someone's life is poorer than another's, Sen leaves the question to be settled through processes of public reasoning, that is, different viewpoints coming together in order to find common agreements (Sen 2017).

Like Sen's works, religious traditions have also sought to deal with the normative questions at the core of development regarding what constitutes a good or 'better' life and which social arrangements and outcomes are better than others. This book has selected the Roman Catholic tradition as the conversation partner. It has chosen such a focus because this particular religious tradition has developed over the last 130 years a body of texts which discuss, from a normative perspective, socio-economic and political issues, and which, since 1963, has been addressed to every person of goodwill, of all faiths, and none. Catholicism is also the denomination with the largest number of adherents within the Christian religion, which is the largest religious group, followed by Islam and Hinduism.[13] It is also of particular importance in Latin America, from where many of the illustrative examples of this book have been drawn.

The Christian social tradition goes back to the practice of early faith communities that cared for the sick, the hungry, the widows, the orphans, and the marginalized groups of the time, and it has developed to this day, if often in less than adequate ways.[14] In the late nineteenth century, the publication of *Rerum Novarum* (RN, *On New Things*) by Pope Leo XIII marked a new departure within the Catholic Church with its constructive analysis of distinctly modern socio-economic realities from the perspective of the Gospel. *Rerum Novarum* discussed how to respond to the 'new things' that the world was experiencing with the Industrial Revolution and the exploitation of factory workers. It pressed on governments to legislate for minimum wages and labour rights, such as protection against illness and accidents. It also affirmed the right of workers to form unions.[15]

Since then, subsequent popes have issued documents that expanded on the analysis of their predecessors, given the new realities they were facing. To name a few:[16] as the Cold War was settling in, Pope John XXIII issued *Pacem in Terris* (*Peace on Earth*) in 1963; during the first UN Development Decade and after decolonization in many countries, Pope Paul VI issued *Populorum Progressio* (*On the Progress of Peoples*) in 1967; as Latin American dictatorships were coming to an end in the 1980s and a communist system was in place in Eastern Europe and elsewhere, Pope John Paul II issued *Sollicitudo Rei Socialis* (SRS, *On Social Concerns*) in 1987; as the world was dealing with the socio-economic consequences of a global financial crisis, Pope Benedict XVI issued *Caritas in Veritate* (CV, *Charity in Truth*) in 2009; as the devastating effects of climate change and the limits of certain models of development or progress based on infinite economic growth and resource exploitation became more pressing, Pope Francis issued *Laudato Si': On Care for our Common Home* (LS) in June 2015, breaking with the century-long tradition of naming papal documents (encyclicals) by their first two words in Latin;[17] and as national populist political systems had advanced in many democracies, Pope Francis issued *Fratelli Tutti* (FT, *Brothers and Sisters All*) in October 2020, whose title also comes from St Francis of Assisi.

This book will focus on the encyclicals that deal more specifically with reflections on socio-economic progress and global justice (namely *Populorum Progressio*, *Sollicitudo Rei Socialis*, *Caritas in Veritate*, *Laudato Si'*, and *Fratelli Tutti*). These documents constitute what is known as Catholic social teaching. In addition, the book will refer to wider reflections on socio-economic matters that are emerging from the whole body of the Catholic Church, such as academic work, and responses of faith communities on the ground to the socio-economic processes they are experiencing.[18] These broadly form what is known as the Catholic social tradition. The Catholic Church's social analysis has a dynamic character. It seeks to respond to novel circumstances, starting from the perspective of the conclusions of past analysis and then taking them to new contexts. As the next chapters will discuss, what started as 'integral human development' as the Catholic Church's vision of development in the 1960s in response to decolonization and the UN Development Decade has evolved today towards 'integral ecology' in response to the climate emergency.

The theoretical and conceptual discussion of the next chapters is accompanied by illustrative examples drawn mainly from the Amazon region and other contexts of socio-environmental degradation. The Amazon region is a place where a process has already begun for translating the conclusions of *Laudato Si'* into actions at the social, economic, social, political, cultural, and ecclesial levels. This process has started with a Special Assembly of all the bishops of the Amazon region, delegations of indigenous peoples, representatives of civil society organizations, and pastoral workers to discuss the current situation in the region and discern new paths for an integral ecology. The Assembly, known as the Amazon Synod, took place in Rome in October 2019.[19] The Amazon region also plays an essential role in the world's ecosystems (Hubau et al. 2020; Nagy et al. 2016; Nobre et al. 2016) and is a paradigmatic illustration of what is happening elsewhere, such as in the Congo basin and the rivers and forests of the Asia-Pacific region.

This book is written with a range of disciplinary and professional audiences in mind: the disciplinary audiences of development studies, theology, and religious studies, and the professional audiences of teachers, researchers, postgraduate students, and workers in development organizations. It aims to cater for readers wanting to engage with the human development and capability approach literature and for those interested in the Catholic social tradition. The book is structured around three areas: the concept and meaning of development (Chapter 1); its underlying conception of being human (Chapter 2); and pathways for transformation (Chapter 3). Each chapter is structured in a similar way. It starts by discussing the perspective of Amartya Sen's capability approach to development; it then examines the perspective of the Catholic social tradition and its contributions. It concludes with some critical remarks on points of tension and pending agendas in the conversation. In its striving to offer a critical engagement between 'secular' and 'religious' understandings of development for a mixed audience, the book will seek to avoid development and theological jargon. However, the reader will have to bear with the unavoidable key development studies concept of 'capability' and the unavoidable Catholic social tradition concept of 'integral', which the next chapter unpacks.

Notes

1 See, among others, Barrera (2019), Clarke and Jennings (2007), Clarke (2013), Koehrsen and Heuser (2020), Marshall and van Saanen (2007). See also the special issue on 'faith-based health care', *The Lancet*, 7 July 2015 (vol. 386, no. 10005), and the special issue on 'Faith and health in development contexts', *Development in Practice*, July 2017 (vol. 27, no. 5).

2 Taken from https://sdgs.un.org/goals, accessed 5 January 2021.

3 See also the conference on Religions and the Sustainable Development Goals held in March 2019 at the Vatican, www.humandevelopment.va/en/eventi/2019/religions-and-the-sustainable-development-goals-7-9-marzo-2019.html, accessed 5 January 2021.

4 See www.partner-religion-development.org/about/vision-and-structure, accessed 5 January 2021. The partnership is funded by the German Federal Ministry for Economic Cooperation and Development (BMZ) and the United States Agency for International Development (USAID).

5 See Fukuda-Parr and McNeill (2019), Pogge and Sengupta (2016), Sachs (2017), Spangenberg (2017).

6 For the urgency of addressing climate change, see the reports of the Intergovernmental Panel on Climate Change at www.ipcc.ch/, and the sixth synthesis report on climate change scheduled in 2022. The report on impacts and adaptation is set to be released in October 2021, see www.ipcc.ch/report/sixth-assessment-report-working-group-ii/, accessed 5 January 2021.

7 See the July 2020 report of the United Nations Environment Programme on 'Preventing the next pandemic – Zoonotic diseases and how to break the chain of transmission' at www.unenvironment.org/resources/report/preventing-future-zoonotic-disease-outbreaks-protecting-environment-animals-and, accessed 5 January 2021.

8 In the UK, see www.buildbackbetteruk.org. The Vatican has set up a special Covid-19 commission to prepare the future: www.humandevelopment.va/en/vatican-covid-19.html. The OECD set up a policy response team: www.oecd.org/coronavirus/policy-responses/building-back-better-a-sustainable-resilient-recovery-after-covid-19-52b869f5, accessed 5 January 2021.

9 For the transformational character of development and its seeking of making situations better, see Arsal and Dasgupta (2015) and Sumner and Tribe (2008).

10 The category 'developing' has been intensely debated; see, for example, https://blogs.worldbank.org/opendata/should-we-continue-use-term-developing-world; www.qeh.ox.ac.uk/content/what-do-we-mean-development-studies-reflections-after-20-years-mphil, accessed 5 January 2021.

11 See the statement of the UK Development Studies Association at www.devstud.org.uk/about/what-is-development-studies, accessed 5 January 2021.

12 See www.hdr.undp.org.

13 In 2018, there was an estimated 1.329 billion people baptized in the Catholic Church, or about 18 per cent of the global population; see www.laciviltacattolica.com/church-numbers-in-the-world (accessed 5 January 2021). In 2010, according to Pew Forum data, 15 per cent of the world's population was estimated to be Hindu, 23.2 per cent Muslim and 31.5 per cent Christian; see www.pewforum.org/2012/12/18/global-religious-landscape-exec, accessed 5 January 2021.

14 For a discussion on the writings of the early Church and implications for contemporary social ethics, see Brown (2014) and Leemans, Matz and Verstraeten (2011). For a discussion of contemporary faith communities taking care of the sick, the hungry, and the marginalized, see Calderisi (2013).

15 For an introduction to Catholic social teaching, see Dorr (2016), Hornsby-Smith (2006), and PCJP (2005).

16 A list of all the documents of Catholic Social Teaching till 2015 can be found at www.usccb.org/beliefs-and-teachings/what-we-believe/catholic-social-teaching/

foundational-documents, accessed 5 January 2020. For a discussion on how each document responds to the socio-economic context of the time, see Catta (2015, 2019), Dorr (2016).

17 The title *Laudato Si'* comes from the Canticle of St Francis of Assisi in Old Italian 'Praise Be to You'.

18 See Ivereigh (2010), Verstraeten (2013), and Mich (1998) for a discussion of the interaction between the social action of faith communities and the Catholic social tradition and their mutual upbuilding.

19 See www.sinodoamazonico.va/content/sinodoamazonico/en.html, accessed 5 January 2021.

References

Alff, Henryk and Anna-Katharina Hornidge. 2019. "Transformation in International Development Studies: Across Disciplines, Knowledge Hierarchies and Oceanic Spaces," in Elisabetta Basile, Isa Baud, Tina Kontinen and Susanne von Itter (eds), *Building Development Studies for the New Millennium*, New York: Palgrave Macmillan, pp. 141–61.

Arsal, Murat and Anirban Dasgupta. 2015. "Critique, Rediscovery and Revival in Development Studies," *Development and Change* 47(4): 644–65, https://doi.org/10.1111/dech.12183.

Barrera, Albino. 2019. *Catholic Missionaries and Their Work with the Poor*, Abingdon: Routledge.

Brown, Peter. 2014. *Through the Eye of a Needle: Wealth, the Fall of Rome, and the Making of Christianity in the West, 350–550 AD*, Princeton: Princeton University Press.

Calderisi, Robert. 2013. *Earthly Mission: The Catholic Church and World Development*, New Haven: Yale University Press.

Catta, Grégoire. 2015. "'God For Us' in the Challenge of Integral Human Development: Theology in Post-Vatican II Catholic Social Teaching," PhD, Massachusetts: Boston College.

———. 2019. *Catholic Social Teaching as Theology*, Mahwah, NJ: Paulist Press.

Clarke, Gerard and Michael Jennings (eds). 2007. *Development, Civil Society and Faith-Based Organisations*, Basingstoke: Palgrave Macmillan.

Clarke, Matthew (ed). 2013. *Handbook of Research on Development and Religion*, Northampton, MA: Edward Elgar.

Dorr, Donal. 2016. *Option for the Poor and for the Earth*, Revised edition, Maryknoll, NY: Orbis.

Fukuda-Parr, Sakiko and Desmond McNeill. 2019. "Knowledge and Politics in Setting and Measuring the SDGs: Introduction to Special Issue," *Global Policy* 10(Suppl. 1): 5–15, https://doi.org/10.1111/1758-5899.12604.

Horner, Rory and David Hulme. 2019. "From International to Global Development: New Geographies of 21st Century Development," *Development and Change* 50(2): 347–78, https://doi.org/10.1111/dech.12379.

Hornsby-Smith, Michael. 2006. *An Introduction to Catholic Social Thought*, Cambridge: Cambridge University Press.

Hubau, Wannes et al. 2020. "Asynchronous Carbon Sink Saturation in African and Amazonian Tropical Forests," *Nature* 579(7797): 80–7, www.nature.com/articles/s41586-020-2035-0.

International Panel on Social Progress (IPSP). 2018. *Rethinking Society for the 21st Century*, Cambridge: Cambridge University Press, www.ipsp.org.

Ivereigh, Austen. 2010. *Faithful Citizens: A Practical Guide to Catholic Social Teaching and Community Organising*, London: Darton, Longman and Todd.

Koehrsen, Jens and Andreas Heuser (eds). 2020. *Faith-Based Organizations in Development Discourses and Practice*, Abingdon: Routledge.

Leemans, Johan, Brian Matz and Johan Verstraeten. 2011. *Reading Patristic Texts on Social Ethics: Issues and Challenges for Twenty-First-Century Christian Social Thought*, Washington, DC: Catholic University of America Press.

Marshall, K. and M. Van Saanen. 2007. *Development and Faith*, Washington, DC: World Bank.

Mich, Marvin L. Krier. 1998. *Catholic Social Teaching and Movements*, Mystic, CT: Twenty-Third Publications.

Nagy, Lazlo, Bruce Forsberg and Paulo Artaxo (eds). 2016. *Interactions Between Biosphere, Atmosphere and Human Land Use in the Amazon Basin*, Berlin, Heidelberg: Springer.

Narayan, Deepa et al. 2000. *Voices of the Poor: Crying out for Change*, New York: Oxford University Press, http://hdl.handle.net/10986/13848.

Nobre, Carlos et al. 2016. "Land-Use and Climate Change Risks in the Amazon and the Need of a Novel Sustainable Development Paradigm," *Proceedings of the National Academy of Sciences of the United States of America* 113(39): 10759–68, doi: 10.1073/pnas.1605516113.

Nunan, Fiona (ed). 2017. *Making Climate Compatible Development Happen*, London: Routledge.

Oswald, Katie, Melissa Leach and John Gaventa. 2019. " 'Engaged Excellence in Development Studies," in Elisabetta Basile, Isa Baud, Tina Kontinen and Susanne von Itter (eds), *Building Development Studies for the New Millennium*, New York: Palgrave Macmillan, pp. 119–39.

Petersen, Marie Juul and Ben Jones. 2011. "Instrumental, Narrow, Normative? Reviewing Recent Work on Religion and Development," *Third World Quarterly* 32(7): 1291–306, https://doi.org/10.1080/01436597.2011.596747.

Pogge, Thomas and Mitu Sengupta. 2016. "Assessing the Sustainable Development Goals from a Human Rights Perspective," *Journal of International and Comparative Social Policy* 32(2): 83–97, https://doi.org/10.1080/21699763.2016.1198268.

Pontifical Council for Justice and Peace (PCJP). 2005. *Compendium of the Social Doctrine of the Church*, www.vatican.va/roman_curia/pontifical_councils/justpeace/documents/rc_pc_justpeace_doc_20060526_compendio-dott-soc_en.html.

Rist, Gilbert. 2014. *The History of Development: From Western Origins to Global Faith*, 4th edition, London: Zed Books.

Robeyns, Ingrid. 2017. *Wellbeing, Freedom and Social Justice: The Capability Approach Re-Examined*, Cambridge: Open Book Publishers, www.openbookpublishers.com/product/682.

Sachs, Wolfgang. 2017. "The Sustainable Development Goals and Laudato Si': Varieties of Post-Development?" *Third World Quarterly* 38(12): 2573–88, https://doi.org/10.1080/01436597.2017.1350822.

Schöneberg, Julia. 2019. "Imagining Postcolonial Development Studies," in Elisabetta Basile, Isa Baud, Tina Kontinen and Susanne von Itter (eds), *Building Development Studies for the New Millennium*, New York: Palgrave Macmillan, pp. 97–116.

Sen, Amartya. 1977. "Rational Fools: A Critique of the Behavioral Foundations of Economic Theory," *Philosophy & Public Affairs* 6(4): 317–44, doi: 10.2307/2264946.

———. 1985. "Well-being, Agency and Freedom: The Dewey Lectures 1984," *Journal of Philosophy* 82(4): 169–221, doi: 10.2307/2026184.

———. 1993. "Capability and Well-Being," in M. Nussbaum and A. Sen (eds), *The Quality of Life*, Oxford: Clarendon Press, pp. 30–53.

———. 2017. *Collective Choice and Social Welfare*, London: Allen Lane.

Spangenberg, Joachim H. 2017. "Hot Air or Comprehensive Progress? A Critical Assessment of the SDGs," *Sustainable Development* 25(4): 311–21, https://doi.org/10.1002/sd.1657.

Sumner, Andy and Michael Tribe. 2008. "What could Development Studies be?" *Development in Practice* 18(6): 755–66, doi: 10.1080/09614520802386603.

Tomalin, Emma. 2020. "Global Aid and Faith Actors: The Case for an Actor-Orientated Approach to the 'Turn to Religion'," *International Affairs* 96(2): 323–42, https://doi.org/10.1093/ia/iiaa006.

Tomalin, Emma, Jörg Haustein and Shabaana Kidy. 2019. "Religion and the Sustainable Development Goals," *The Review of Faith & International Affairs* 17(2): 102–18, https://doi.org/10.1080/15570274.2019.1608664.

Verstraeten, Johan. 2013. "Catholic Social Thought and the Movements: Towards Social Discernment and a Transformative Presence in the World," *Journal of Catholic Social Thought* 10(2): 231–9, https://doi.org/10.5840/jcathsoc201310212.

Wuppertal Conference on Eco-Theology and the Ethics of Sustainability. 2019. *Kairos for Creation: Confessing Hope for the Earth. The "Wuppertal Call"*, Solingen: Foedus-verlag, https://repository.globethics.net/handle/20.500.12424/3863482.

Ziai, Aram. 2017. "Post-Development 25 Years after the Development Dictionary," *Third World Quarterly* 38(12): 2547–58, https://doi.org/10.1080/01436597.2017.1383853.

1 The concept of development

Sen's capability approach to development

When Amartya Sen introduced the term 'capability' to the academic literature in his *Tanner Lectures in Human Values* delivered at the University of
Stanford in 1979 (Sen 1980), he did not realize the extent to which it would
take on a life of its own years later.[1] Today, hundreds of students throughout
the world are conducting master's and doctoral dissertations using what
is now known as the capability approach in fields as varied as education,
philosophy, sociology, politics, economics, geography, law, engineering,
and theology.[2] The *Human Development Reports*, published annually since
1990 by the UNDP, have served as a main vehicle to bring the ideas of the
capability approach into wider academic and policy circles, as has Sen's
book *Development as Freedom*, published in 1999 and based on a series of
lectures he delivered at the World Bank (Sen 1999).

The literature on the capability approach is now vast. Dozens of books
and hundreds of articles have been written, including those which are now
considered to be classic works. These include *Commodities and Capabilities* (Sen 1985a), *Inequality Re-Examined* (Sen 1992), the edited collection *The Quality of Life* (Sen and Nussbaum 1993), *Women and Human
Development* (Nussbaum 2000), *Creating Capabilities: The Human Development Project* (Nussbaum 2011), *Valuing Freedoms* (Alkire 2002), *The
Capability Approach: Concepts, Measures and Applications* (Comim,
Alkire and Qizilbash 2008), and the recent *Cambridge Handbook of the
Capability Approach* (Chiappero-Martinetti, Osmani and Qizilbash 2020).
These books provide a state-of-the-art overview of key topics and policy
areas analysed through the lens of the capability approach. The open-access
book *Wellbeing, Freedom and Social Justice: The Capability Approach Re-
Examined* (Robeyns 2017) is one of the most comprehensive accounts of
what the capability approach is, what it is not, and what it has been used for.

DOI: 10.4324/9781003121534-2

Given the existing literature, it would be somewhat redundant to provide an overview of what the capability approach is and the distinctive vision it offers for thinking about development. Sen's classic article 'The concept of development' (Sen 1988) offers an excellent introduction in that regard. Yet there has been little discussion so far of Sen's capability approach and its contributions for thinking about the concept of development from within the context of dialogue with religious traditions.[3] This section highlights some key features of the approach that make it a well-suited conversation partner for dialoguing with religious traditions on development concerns: its assessment of development in the kinds of lives that people live, its open-endedness as an evaluative framework, and its attention to the marginalized.

The kinds of lives that people live

Robeyns (2017: 24) summarizes the capability approach as a 'conceptual framework for a range of evaluative exercises'. What Sen has argued for is to broaden the informational basis on which situations are assessed. Information about 'utility', often reduced to information about income and consumption, had long been the dominant criterion in economics to evaluate situations and rank them according to which one is better or worse. Reducing the informational basis to income would, for example, lead to the assessment that an indigenous family that lives in an informal settlement of the Amazonian city of Manaus and makes an income of 100 US dollars per month is better off than a family that lives in the rainforest and has no monetary income. Such evaluation does not take into account whether the latter may have access to clean water from a river or to food through the forest, and the former no access to clean water or a healthy diet.

Sen has also strongly criticized the so-called criterion of 'Pareto optimality', which is central to utilitarian economics, and according to which a situation is optimal if it is no longer possible to increase the utility of some without decreasing the utility of others. As he notes, using only information about utility could lead to the conclusion that an economy is doing well

> when some people are rolling in luxury and others are near starvation as long as the starvers cannot be made better off without cutting into the pleasures of the rich. . . . [A] society or an economy can be Pareto optimal and still be perfectly disgusting.
>
> (Sen 2017: 68–9).

Introducing information about the kinds of lives that people live would yield different conclusions about how well an economy or society is doing. This has been one of Sen's main contributions in thinking about what counts as development, or what constitutes good change. It is because of this concern for the kinds of lives that people live that he introduces the concept of capabilities.

Considerations about incomes may be important, but they should not be the only sources of information to use when assessing the kinds of lives that people live. Sen argues for judging how well societies are doing 'in terms of what people are able to be or able to do, rather than in terms of the means or resources they possess' (Sen 2017: 357). What people are able to be and do are what he calls 'capabilities'. This concept is closely linked to that of 'functionings', which are simply people's 'beings' and 'doings', such as being in good health, participating in the life of the community, being well nourished, making decisions about one's life, travelling, pursuing education, meeting other people, and so on. A capability is 'the set of combination of functionings from which the person can choose any one combination' or 'the actual freedom of choice a person has over the alternative lives that he or she can lead' (Sen 2017: 357).

Readers familiar with Sen's works would have heard oftentimes the example of the fasting monk and starving child, to illustrate how the concepts of functioning and capability are connected. Both show the same functioning deficit in that both experience being malnourished but one has the capability to be well nourished and the other does not, that is, the fasting monk has a choice of an alternative life he could lead but the starving child does not. For the capability approach to development, both types of information – functionings and capabilities – are equally important for evaluating how people's lives are doing but often, given practical considerations, data availability and relevance, it is information about the kinds of lives that people live – whether they are adequately sheltered, adequately nourished, are in good health, and so on – rather than their actual freedom over alternative lives that will be the primary concern (Sen 1992).[4] It would make little sense to assess how well the lives of residents of an informal settlement are doing by looking at whether their living in a neighbourhood with high level of violence and inadequate services and infrastructure (such as unsafe gas connections, broken sewage, and no waste collection) is a choice or not. There may be a difference between a family that has chosen to live in such a neighbourhood because of the close-knit social networks and one which has not because it cannot afford to live in a safer neighbourhood. For the purpose of assessing how people in the neighbourhood live, information about people's functionings is more relevant than information about their capability set, in the sense of their actual freedom of choice over the alternative lives they can lead, to paraphrase Sen. Such choice has also been referred to by Sen as a person's agency, which he defines as 'the pursuit of whatever goals or values he or she regards as important' (Sen 1985b: 203). In the example here, the family that has chosen to live in an informal settlement despite being able to afford to live in a better neighbourhood is considered to have exercised agency – that is, pursuing something they regard as important, such as living in a close-knit community despite the poor conditions of public services in the neighbourhood.

It would however be a misinterpretation to conclude that Sen's capability approach conceives of development as being about human freedom, as suggested by his book title *Development as Freedom* (Sen 1999). He once commented that 'development as freedom' was just the title of one book – which his publisher chose – and not a summary of his arguments about the concept of development.[5] His concern for human freedom has to be put in its context, which is broadening the informational basis for evaluating states of affairs beyond information about utility (Sen 1970). It would also be misinterpretation to conclude that Sen's capability approach is about choices, which is how the *Human Development Reports* translated the term 'capabilities' until recently.[6] What can appear as a choice may not be as much the result of the exercise of human freedom as the result of indirect coercion. For example, for workers to work for less than the minimum wage may appear to be a 'choice', but the workers may have no other alternative than work in these conditions. As Sen (2017: 177) puts it, '[w]orkers may agree to accept sub-human wages and poor terms of employment, since in the absence of a contract they may starve, but this does not make that solution a desirable outcome in any sense'. Outcomes, that is, the actual lives that people live, matter too. A person could choose to work for below the minimum wage out of solidarity with those who cannot find better paid employment,[7] but this does not make these employment conditions desirable even if she has chosen them when alternatives were available.

One can already see, in this feature of Sen's capability approach to development, why it has a special resonance for religious traditions. It puts a similar emphasis on the centrality of the human person, of her inalienable dignity and her flourishing, as the ultimate end of socio-economic processes (PCJP 2005: 108–14). The inclusion of agency gives space to account for the pursuit of the objectives one values, especially in relation to changing situations which undermine human dignity or destroy nature, even at the cost of one's own well-being, and sometimes one's own life, such as for those who have chosen to continue denouncing illegal deforestation in the Amazon in the face of death threats rather than remain silent.[8] Here, as will be discussed later, the Catholic social tradition would refer to solidarity, commitment to the common good, or 'the way of love' (PCJP 2005: 205–8).

An open-ended framework for evaluation

Sen has strongly objected to his contributions to questions of development being reduced to the capability approach. When he first proposed the idea of capabilities in his *Tanner Lectures* in 1979 (Sen 1980), it was in response to the limits of utility, income, and resources to provide an answer to the question of how one's life is going. Something else was needed, and he called it 'capabilities'. Never did he imagine then that the concept would 'escalate' the way it has today. It was about 'opening up a line of thinking'. His intention was not to create a school of thought, or a scholarly community, around the capability approach.[9] To the question whether he was a 'capability theorist', he vehemently replied in the negative:

> Capability is not a formula, 'it's pointing towards a certain space'. . . . I'm saying this – the capability space – is a relevant space in a way that the utility space is not, the commodity space is not. That's it.
>
> (Sen quoted in Baujard and Gilardone 2017: 7)

Sen (2017: 358) has also cautioned against using information about capabilities or functionings as the sole criterion for assessing development. The informational basis can be extended to how ecosystems are doing and how well they are functioning, for example, whether the spotted owl is at risk of extinction and how well it is doing (Sen 2004), and to considerations about processes beyond outcomes, for example, whether nobody has been intimidated or coerced into doing or being something.

In some ways, one could infer from Sen's own statements that talking of Sen's capability approach to development is a misinterpretation of his original intentions, as he never intended to propose 'a capability approach' in order to think about questions of development, progress, and social change. His intention was to open up a line of thinking that displaces the primacy of income growth when thinking about these questions and to point out that considerations about what people are able to do and be matter and should not be lost amidst considerations about growth of economic output. Sen's argument may be a statement of the obvious for many, but there is no dearth of examples of situations where human lives continue to be lost amidst considerations of growth of economic output. In Latin America, the agribusiness and mining sectors, which have strongly been supported by government policies through tax incentives, have often left those who live in the regions of their business operations with worsened quality of life, especially in the area of health, and in some cases have led to deaths caused by pesticide poisoning or mine wastewater contamination. Soya production, which has brought higher levels of economic output in Paraguay, has been particularly damaging for people's health (Correia 2019; Ezquerro-Cañete 2016),[10] as has mining in Peru, Argentina, and elsewhere (Svampa 2019; Valencia 2016); it is estimated that about 50 per cent of the population and 64 per cent children of the Peruvian Amazon show higher levels of mercury in their blood' beyond the maximum health level, and 64 per cent of children do (UNDP 2020: 68).

While putting people and their flourishing at the centre of socio-economic processes, Sen's capability approach remains open-ended regarding what human flourishing might entail. He has left the matter of what a good, or flourishing, human life is open to debate. He uses, instead, open-ended expressions such as 'freedoms that people have reason to value' (Sen 1992: 81) and has famously abstained from specifying which valuable capabilities, or functionings, should constitute the benchmark against which development or progress is to be assessed, as the selection depends on what is being evaluated and for what purposev (Robeyns 2017). An example could be the challenge in comparing a situation where people in an informal settlement have a brick house with piped water, a separate kitchen, and a bathroom with a situation where a house is built with less durable material and poor sanitary conditions but has the potential to be extended to accommodate future family needs. The conclusion will depend on the context and aim of the evaluation exercise. If the aim is to evaluate a government housing programme in an informal settlement, then the relevant functioning to consider may need to be different from simply living in a house with piped water. Frediani (2015) tells the story of a housing programme in Brazil which assumed that what people valued was living in a solid house with a kitchen and a bathroom. However, the programme failed because it did not take into account a functioning the residents valued – that of living in a house they could extend. The prefabricated houses provided by the government started to crack when people began to build extensions for their expanding families, and the residents soon abandoned their new houses to go back to the shacks they could extend. In contrast, if the aim of the evaluation is to assess poverty at the global level, the functioning of 'living in a house with access to piped water and a solid floor' is more relevant than that of living in a house one can extend.[11]

Within the literature on the capability approach, there have been many discussions about the specification of valuable functionings/capabilities and a division between what is perceived as Sen's version, which is open-ended, and Martha Nussbaum's version, which specifies a list of central human capabilities (Nussbaum 2000, 2011).[12] According to Robeyns (2017), this division reflects different aims and uses of the approach and is not about two different versions. Nussbaum's aim is to develop a theory of justice, similar to that of John Rawls, with the difference that his list of primary goods is replaced with a list of central human capabilities to inform redistributive principles. Sen's aim is not to offer a theory of justice, but an evaluative framework to compare states of affairs as a basis for thinking about questions of development and redistribution.

This open-endedness of Sen's capability approach to development creates a space for spiritual considerations to be included. For example, the functioning of being in relation to a higher source of value, or being in relation to one's ancestors, land, and animals, could be included in the evaluation of how well a country is doing. For example, Bhutan has included spirituality within the dimension of psychological well-being in its Gross National Happiness Index.[13] Different societies will hold different value judgements about which information should be included or excluded in the evaluation of how well their societies are doing given their contexts, but this raises questions about who decides what is important and how such value judgements are made.

The centrality of value judgments within Sen's capability approach to development goes together with a dynamic perspective on values. Different values do not only co-exist alongside each other but also interact and change as a result of interaction. There is also a strong connection between values and policy changes. Policies change when what people regard as important changes. Discussing the threats of climate change and environmental degradation, Sen highlights the role of value formation in changing policies:

> The [environmental] threats that we face call for organized international action as well as changes in national policies. . . . But they are also dependent on value formation, related to public discussions, both for their influence on individual behaviour and for bringing about policy changes – through political processes.
>
> (Sen 2017: 40)

In that regard, religious traditions have contributions to make to wider public debates on values. How a religious tradition values, for example, an animal species, not as something to serve human needs, but as something that has value in itself, could contribute to public debates on the protection of biodiversity.[14] On the question as to why an endangered animal species should be protected, such as the spotted owl, Sen (2004) alludes to the reason the Buddhist tradition gives, namely that 'since we are enormously more powerful than other species, we have some responsibility towards them that is linked with this asymmetry' (Sen 2004: 11). However, for Sen, these values are to be critically examined, scrutinized, and vigorously debated with others (Sen 2017: 39, 281), especially in the light of what is happening to the lives of the most vulnerable.

Attention to human suffering and to the marginalized

Sen's capability approach proposes a concept of development that bridges the global South/global North or developing/developed country divide. It offers a framework for evaluative exercises in many different contexts – for example, from assessing how an East London borough is doing, and whether its residents live better lives in 2020 than they did in 2010, to assessing how an entire country is doing. The approach has fed into policy evaluation frameworks such as the OECD's *How's Life?* (OECD 2013) and the New Zealand government's *Living Standards Framework* (Hall 2019), in addition to offering alternatives to gross domestic product measures such as the Human Development Index and its related family of indices.[15]

In the midst of the multiple uses to which the capability approach has been put, such as to think differently about education (McGrath 2018; Walker and Unterhalter 2007), disability (Mitra 2016; Terzi 2020), gender equality (Agarwal, Humphries and Robeyns 2008), and health (Venkatapuram 2011), attention to human suffering, to those who are marginalized and disadvantaged, has been a running theme throughout Sen's works and in applications of his capability approach. It is probably not a biographical underestimation to say that the Bengal famine of 1943 that Sen lived through as a ten-year old boy had a long-lasting imprint on his intellectual work, such as his childhood experience of finding a stabbed Muslim man at the door or of sharing some rice in the school grounds with children from families who were affected by the famine (Sen 2015; Hamilton 2019). It is around that time that Sen read the story of the life of Buddha which also inspired him and influenced his later works (Sen 2014). Among these influences, he highlights human suffering as a starting point for reflection and action, non-parochialism (the sufferings of the distant others do not matter less than those in immediate surroundings), and dialogue and reasoning as key for taking actions to remove suffering.

A consequence of situating the objective of development in enabling people to live good lives – or to put it in Sen's terms, to live lives that they have reason to value – is the policy concern of identifying and responding to shortfalls in the ability to live such lives. Sen's concept of development may be summarized as 'development as capability expansion' (Sen 2003), but it is reducing 'capability deprivation' – that is, 'a lack of opportunity to lead a minimally acceptable life' (Sen 2017: 26) – which is its main policy concern. Characteristically, Sen leaves the issue of what counts as a 'minimally acceptable life' open-ended, stating that it involves 'elementary functionings', such as 'being alive, being well-nourished, and in good health, moving about freely', and 'more complex functionings', such as 'having self-respect and respect for others, and taking part in the life of the community' (Sen 2017: 357).[16]

Many initiatives are currently being undertaken worldwide to identify and measure deficits in leading such a 'minimally acceptable life'. At the global level, a Multidimensional Poverty Index considers shortfalls in the dimensions of health, education, and standard of living.[17] The difference between measuring poverty in terms of income (those living on less than $1.90 per day) and capability deprivation can in some countries be significant.[18] At the national level, multidimensional poverty measures have been developed to reflect national contexts, such as the inclusion of freedom of movement as an indicator of capability deprivation in Palestine[19] or crime incidence and physical safety in El Salvador.[20] There is also research on developing multidimensional poverty measures in urban settings using indicators of capability deprivation in housing, health, education, employment, and safety (Mitchell and Maccio 2018).

The idea of capability was introduced in the context of the question 'Equality of what?' If one is concerned about equality, about every person being granted equal dignity by virtue of her birth, in which space should equality be measured? Sen's answer to that question was that the space of functionings/capabilities is more appropriate than that of income. The moral problem is not so much that one person in one country may earn 100 dollars a month and another 10,000 but that the person who earns only 100 dollars may not have the same opportunity to live in decent accommodation; be adequately nourished; afford decent healthcare; and have quality education, time to relax, and play; receive attention in courts; or enjoy other valuable functionings. The development of a multidimensional inequality index, which would complement income inequality indices, is still work in progress (Anand et al. 2020; Seth and Santos 2020; Vizard and Speed 2016). It is within the concern for human suffering and the marginalized and disadvantaged – in other words, concern for those who are unable to live a 'minimal acceptable life' – that income inequality, and having too much income, is a moral problem that needs to be addressed. In examining what might be wrong with extreme wealth within the normative evaluative framework of the capability approach, Robeyns (2019) argues that extreme wealth is not morally justifiable because it undermines the democratic process, with the wealthiest people influencing policies for their own advantage,[21] and because high-consumption lifestyles linked to extreme wealth further accelerate climate change and in consequence further damage the lives of the most vulnerable.[22] She also makes the argument that climate justice requires a shift of resources towards low-carbon technologies and that there is therefore a moral justification for reorienting excess wealth to that end.

Putting the concern for the marginalized, and the human person and her flourishing, as the objective of development has been Amartya Sen's main contribution to discussions on the concept and meaning of development. Development is about 'human development'; it is about humans living in dignity and enjoying a 'minimally acceptable life'. There have been many critiques of Sen's work, and this present chapter may appear to the reader to be one among such 'hagiographic renditions of his work' (Fischer 2018: 131). There are critiques that the idea of capability is a confusing and 'beguiling concept' (Dean 2009), that it focuses excessively on freedom with its end never questioned and its assumption that freedoms never conflict (Corbridge 2002) – such as the freedom to be healthy and the freedom to travel to work or socialize with others in Covid times, that there is far too much optimism in the reach of what human reason can achieve and an underappreciation of power dynamics (Hamilton 2019), that it does not help us to understand structural transformation and how social change happens (Fischer 2018), that it does not question the neoliberal economic order (Bagchi 2000), and that it is too human-centred (and individual-centred) and may not be able to incorporate views that see humans as part of a wider web of life as is found in indigenous cosmologies (Van Jaarsveld 2020; Watene 2016).

Some concerns raised by these critiques will be discussed in later chapters (such as the reach of human reason and its anthropocentrism), but one has to bear in mind that Sen's aim was never to propose a theory of development which would help understand how change happens, how to make it happen, or to propose a comprehensive system for evaluating how well people's lives or societies are doing. What he has proposed is simply an evaluative framework that puts people's lives at the centre, opens up conversations about the ends and means of development, and does so with special attention to the lives of the marginalized. The question remains, therefore, as to what Sen's capability approach to development, as an evaluative framework to assess how people's lives are doing, can offer to the lives of the marginalized. What can it offer to, for example, the Yanomami people in northern Brazil who are being displaced from their land by thousands of illegal gold miners encroaching onto their territory, or to those who live near soya fields in Paraguay affected by pesticides, or to the hundreds of thousands of street vendors in Latin America who have lost their livelihoods due to Covid-19 lockdown restrictions? One could answer that it offers a framework to evaluate the consequences of illegal gold mining for the lives of the Yanomami and the loss of what they value being and doing, or the consequences of soya agribusinesses for the lives of peasant communities, or the consequences of Covid-19 for street vendors' lives. But it does not go beyond evaluation. The next section explores how a religious tradition brings to bear some perspectives that go further than Sen's capability approach to development in that respect.

Integral human development

Soon after the emergence of the development era in the early 1960s, the Catholic Church issued a reflection on the concept of development and the meaning of progress in a document published by Paul VI in 1967, entitled *Populorum Progressio,* or the *Progress of Peoples.* It was based on the experience of development in Latin America, Africa, and Asia. The document was drafted by Dominican priest, theologian, and economist Louis-Joseph Lebret. He had travelled extensively in the newly independent countries to study their economies and had founded in Paris a research centre on economy and humanism which was dedicated to socio-economic analysis from a humanist perspective.[23] *Populorum Progressio* coined, what has become to this day, a term, namely 'integral human development', by which the Catholic social tradition refers to its vision of development. The term has been used ever since, with its meaning evolving with the social context and as new challenges arose. In 2017, Pope Francis created the Dicastery for Promoting Integral Human Development – a dicastery is to Catholic Church governance what a government ministry is to state governance – to replace the Pontifical Council for Justice and Peace, which had been created in the wake of the Second Vatican Council. One could compare the creation of this new Dicastery with the creation of the Human Development Report Office by the UNDP in 1990, an office dedicated to analysing situations globally from the perspective of Sen's capability approach to development and to promoting the approach in policy and practice. The Dicastery for Promoting Integral Human Development has been set

> to promote the integral development of the human person in the light of the Gospel,[24] 'to propose a humanism that is up to the standards of God's plan of love in history, an integral and solidary humanism capable of creating a new social, economic and political order, founded on the dignity and freedom of every human person, to be brought about in peace, justice and solidarity'.[25]

The Catholic social tradition thus does not solely advocate a human development approach like the UNDP but an *integral* one. But what is meant by 'integral'?

Populorum Progressio defines integral human development as follows: 'The development We [*sic*] speak of here cannot be restricted to economic growth alone. To be authentic, it must be well rounded; it must foster the development of each [wo]man and of the whole [wo]man' (PP 14).[26] The original version of the encyclical was written in French, and it reads: 'Le développement ne se réduit pas à la simple croissance économique. Pour être authentique, il doit être intégral, c'est-à-dire promouvoir tout homme et tout l'homme', which would be better translated as 'development cannot be reduced merely to economic growth. To be authentic, it must be integral, that is, promote the development of the person and the whole person.' When John Paul II quotes this definition in *Sollicitudo Rei Socialis*, the word 'integral' was translated as 'complete' (SRS 9).

The word 'integral' is a reference to French philosopher Jacques Maritain's writings on 'Humanisme Intégral', a humanism open to the transcendental dimension, and for which the realm of human affairs and the spiritual realm are autonomous without being separated, each influencing the other (Catta 2015). The wording also derives from the writings of Henri de Lubac on the relation between the 'natural' and the 'supernatural'. He argued that 'a natural desire for the supernatural was built into the very concept of the human' and that humans found their fulfilment in what transcends nature, in communion with God.[27] The French version of *Populorum Progressio* reads:

> C'est un humanisme plénier qu'il faut promouvoir. Qu'est-ce à dire, sinon le développement intégral de tout l'homme et de tous les hommes? . . . Il n'est donc d'humanisme vrai qu'ouvert à l'Absolu, dans la reconnaissance d'une vocation, qui donne l'idée vraie de la vie humaine. Loin d'être la norme dernière des valeurs, l'homme ne se réalise lui-même qu'en se dépassant.
>
> (PP 42)

This can be translated as:

> It is a full humanism that needs to be promoted, that is, the integral development of the whole person and all the people. . . . A true humanism is one that is open to the Absolute, in the recognition of a vocation, which gives to human life its true meaning. Far from being the ultimate standard of values, human persons realise themselves only by going beyond themselves.

Today, 'integral' has acquired the meaning of integration or wholeness. In an address to the participants of a conference celebrating the fiftieth anniversary of *Populorum Progressio*, Pope Francis asked:

> What is meant, today and in the near future, by 'integral development', that is, the development of each man and of the whole man?

In the footsteps of Paul VI, perhaps in the very word *integrate* – so dear to me – we can identify a fundamental direction for the new Dicastery.[28]

In his talk, Pope Francis highlighted the integration of peoples, which implied a 'duty of solidarity which obliges us to seek just ways of sharing, so there may not exist that tragic inequality between those who have too much and those who have nothing', the integration of different dimensions of social and economic life, the integration of the individual and the community, and the integration of 'body and soul' as 'no work of development can truly reach its goal if it does not respect that place in which God is present with us and speaks to our heart'.[29]

This section concentrates on three aspects of this view of integration: the integration of all the dimensions of human life, including the spiritual; the integration of the earth among those suffering and marginalized; and the integration of oneself as the subject of development. The discussion will draw mainly on some central documents of the Catholic social tradition, namely papal encyclicals, and on the lived experiences of marginalized communities that form the ground of the theological reflection contained in these documents.[30] In each aspect, it discusses how such an integral perspective could add to Sen's.

The kinds of lives that people live: integrating the spiritual

Within Sen's capability approach, the central concern of development is the kinds of lives that people live and the opportunities they have to function well as human beings. But it chooses to leave the question of what counts as functioning well as a human being, or what it is to live a 'minimal acceptable life', undetermined, beyond specifying some basic functionings like being healthy, being well nourished, or, indeed, being alive. Religious traditions have been more prescriptive in that regard. For the Catholic social tradition, being open to something beyond oneself is a key dimension of functioning well as a human being. For *Populorum Progressio*, this transcendental or spiritual[31] dimension of human life was about being open to 'values of love and friendship, of prayer and contemplation,' for 'this is what will guarantee man's authentic development – his transition from less than human conditions to truly human ones' (PP 20). Lives that lack access to safe water or adequate food reflect dehumanizing conditions, but lives that lack a capacity for love and friendship and are closed to others and self-centred are no less dehumanizing.

Pope Benedict XVI emphasizes and develops this argument further in *Caritas in Veritate* in 2009. It opens with the statement:

> Charity in truth . . . is the principal driving force behind the authentic development of every person and of all humanity. Love – caritas – is an extraordinary force which leads people to opt for courageous and generous engagement in the field of justice and peace. It is a force that has its origin in God, Eternal Love and Absolute Truth.
>
> (CV 1)

It affirms that ' "Caritas in veritate" is the principle around which the Church's social doctrine turns' (CV 6), and it highlights that the promotion of justice and the common good are forms that express this 'charity in truth', or love, which are of 'of special relevance to the commitment to development in an increasingly globalized society' (CV 6). In other words, a human development that is integral is one which is motivated by and orientated to that 'love in truth', 'to which Jesus Christ bore witness by his earthly life and especially by his death and resurrection' (CV 1). The striving to improve human conditions is incomplete without that orientation to 'love received and given' (CV 5). Pope Benedict XVI continues to argue in *Caritas in Veritate* that 'Development, social well-being, the search for a satisfactory solution to the grave socio-economic problems besetting humanity, all need this truth' (CV 6). For the Catholic social tradition, development cannot be complete when limited only to the material dimension, in the sense of better health conditions, better nutrition, better quality housing, more decent employment, and so forth. It becomes complete, or integral, when it also integrates the interior dimension and the growth in our capacity to give and receive love. As John Paul II had affirmed in *Sollicitudo Rei Socialis*, 'Development which is not only economic must be measured and oriented according to the reality and vocation of man seen in his totality, namely, according to his interior dimension' (SRS 29). This is why, like Paul VI in *Populorum Progressio*, both John Paul II and Benedict XVI talk of integral human development as a 'vocation', as a response to God's calling to love and to express that love towards our brothers and sisters in humanity through our work and lives (CV 1, CV 22, SRS 28–29).

Pope Francis extends this vocation to love in *Laudato Si'* to the non-human creation (LS 85). Integral human development implies growth in our love towards not only fellow human beings but also the entire cosmos. *Laudato Si'* talks of the 'mystical meaning to be found in a leaf, in a mountain trail, in a dewdrop, in a poor person's face' (LS 233), of nature being 'filled with words of love' (LS 225). It sees any person who gives herself out of love to help others and protect nature as a manifestation of the divine.

Any person who lives a life open to the wonders of creation, who lives a sustainable lifestyle, and who works at bringing economic and social processes into harmony with creation is involved in integral human development (LS 225). Such 'social love' is 'part of spirituality' and is 'key to authentic development' (LS 231). In *Fratelli Tutti*, Pope Francis develops this notion of social love or 'social friendship' further as a love that seeks the best for other people's lives, that recognizes the equal worth of every person, and that transcends boundaries (FT 94, 98, 106).

An integral human development perspective gives some direction to the freedom and agency in Sen's capability approach, thus answering some of the critiques that its account of human freedom lacks purpose. From a religious tradition perspective, there are some ways of exercising freedom which are 'better' than others, in the sense of fulfilling more of our humanity, namely the ways which express more love for others and for nature. From Sen's capability approach perspective, there is nothing that allows one to distinguish whether, for example, choosing a diet that is meat-heavy versus one that is more plant-based is better or worse, or whether choosing a kind of life that generates high carbon emissions and electronic waste is better or worse than a kind of life that generates low-carbon emissions and little waste, except the reasoning and self-examination process that the person undertakes to make her decision. An integral human development perspective is more prescriptive in the sense that it brings more elements for consideration in the reasoning process, such as the impact of meat consumption on deforestation, soil erosion, and contamination,[32] or the impact of one's high carbon emissions on climate change, or the impact of one's electronic waste on soil contamination and people's health.[33] These other-related considerations are not absent from Sen's capability approach to development, but they are not explicit – though as the conclusion will discuss, the 2020 *Human Development Report* makes these considerations explicit in the exercise of our freedom, the choices we make, and the actions we take, whether individually or collectively.

In the development studies literature, this spiritual dimension has been accounted for by adding an extra dimension alongside others, such as in Bhutan's Gross National Happiness Index or the 'Light Wheel' approach pioneered by Tearfund (2016) for monitoring and impact evaluation. However, the concept of integral human development is not easily translatable into a user guide, as some development organizations, like Catholic Relief Services, have sought to do (Heinrich et al. 2008). Rather, like Sen's capability approach, it is an analytical lens, a conceptual normative framework, through which social realities are analysed. It is more about opening a distinctive line of thought for thinking about development than proposing a formula for evaluation or blueprint for action.

Integral human development adopts a similar multidimensional perspective to that of Sen's when considering each person: her flourishing in all her dimensions is the ultimate concern of development. It similarly does not specify an exhaustive list of dimensions which constitute human life. These could include, like in Sen's, among others, being healthy, pursuing knowledge, and being able to shape one's life and to participate in the life of the community – what *Populorum Progressio* calls 'being an artisan of one's destiny' (PP 65). However, the Catholic social tradition brings more to the fore the intuitive idea of human dignity, which in many ways echoes the anchoring of Sen's capability approach in human rights.[34] Every person is born with equal dignity. As Pope Francis put it in *Fratelli Tutti*,

> the mere fact that some people are born in places with fewer resources or less development does not justify the fact that they are living with less dignity. . . . Every human being has the right to live with dignity and to develop integrally.
>
> (FT 106–107)

Both reject situations in which 'some people are rolling in luxury and others are near starvation' (Sen 2017: 68–9) on the ground that this violates human dignity. However, the Catholic social tradition goes further than Sen by affirming that living a life in luxury in indifference to the suffering of others is dehumanizing. *Fratelli Tutti* discusses at length in that regard political ideologies which fail to consider those who are in a situation of need as our neighbours towards whom we have responsibilities.

Attention to suffering and marginalization: integrating the earth

Like Sen's perspective, the Catholic social tradition gives priority to those who are unable to live a 'minimally acceptable life', those who are unable to have the basic requirements of human dignity like access to food, water, decent housing or decent work. In the wordings of the Second Vatican Council in 1965:

> The joys and the hopes, the griefs and the anxieties of the [wo]men of this age, especially those who are poor or in any way afflicted, these are the joys and hopes, the griefs and anxieties of the followers of Christ.[35]

In its translation of the Second Vatican Council to its reality, the Latin American Church adopted a 'preferential option for the poor',[36] which Pope John Paul II subsequently put at the core of the Catholic social tradition in his encyclical *Sollicitudo Rei Socialis* in 1987.[37] The original term in Spanish (*opción*) suggests a commitment, a firm and deliberate decision, and not an option in the sense of a choice among others as in English. It is about opting to orient one's life and decisions according to the realities of those who suffer:

> This love of preference for the poor, and the decisions which it inspires in us, cannot but embrace the immense multitudes of the hungry, the needy, the homeless, those without medical care and, above all, those without hope of a better future. It is impossible not to take account of the existence of these realities. . . . [This option] applies equally to our social responsibilities and hence to our manner of living, and to the logical decisions to be made concerning the ownership and use of goods.
>
> (SRS 42)

Sollicitudo Rei Socialis makes a strong connection between the preferential option for the poor and the ownership and use of goods, known as the principle of the 'universal destination of goods' (PCJP 2005: 171–84), according to which the earth is destined for all. Our ownership of goods is therefore not absolute but has to be shared and be at the service of others so that each person can have access to a minimum of conditions that will ensure her development as a human being (FT 118–127). Addressing poverty is essential to integral human development, but addressing extreme wealth is no less important. Already in 1968, *Populorum Progressio* asked a stark question:

> What are less than human conditions? The material poverty of those who lack the bare necessities of life, and the moral poverty of those who are crushed under the weight of their own self-love; oppressive political structures resulting from the abuse of ownership or the improper exercise of power, from the exploitation of the worker or unjust transaction.
>
> (PP 21)

Popes John Paul II, Benedict XVI, and Francis all have continued to emphasize this connection between the two: 'side-by-side with the miseries of underdevelopment, themselves unacceptable, we find ourselves up against a form of superdevelopment, equally inadmissible, because like the former it is contrary to what is good and to true happiness' (SRS 28); 'we have a sort of super-development of a wasteful and consumerist kind which forms an unacceptable contrast with the ongoing situations of dehumanizing deprivation' (CV 22, LS 109). *Populorum Progressio* and *Caritas in Veritate* talk of the 'The scandal of glaring inequalities' (PP 9, CV 22).

From the aforementioned, one can conclude that integrating a spiritual dimension into the concept of development implies a specific way of attending to human suffering and poverty, one which connects the life of a person who lives in poverty with that of the one who lives in plenty. But this is not its only implication. Integral human development also implies integrating what *Laudato Si'* calls, following Boff (1997), 'the cry of the earth and the cry of the poor' (LS 49). For the Catholic social tradition, as it has evolved today, nature is not something that is external to human living, 'as something separate from ourselves or as a mere setting in which we live', something that one can use and control, for '[w]e are part of nature, included in it and thus in constant interaction with it' (LS 139). Attention to the poor and marginalized can therefore not be separated from attention to the earth and from the damage that humans are inflicting on it. As mentioned earlier, integrating a spiritual dimension within development means openness to the values of 'love, friendship' not only with others, especially the poor, but with all of nature, or God's creation.[38]

An integral human development perspective is neither anthropocentric nor biocentric. It sees human beings and ecosystems in constant interaction. Degradation of people's lives and of ecosystems goes hand in hand, as the people consulted for the Amazon Synod expressed:

> The Amazon today is a wounded and deformed beauty, a place of suffering and violence. Attacks on nature have consequences for people's lives . . . appropriation and privatization of natural goods, such as water itself; legal logging concessions and illegal logging; predatory hunting and fishing; unsustainable mega-projects (hydroelectric and forest concessions, massive logging, monocultivation, highways, waterways, railways, and mining and oil projects); pollution caused by extractive industries and city garbage dumps; and, above all, climate change. These are real threats with serious social consequences: pollution-related diseases, drug trafficking, illegal armed groups, alcoholism, violence against women, sexual exploitation, human trafficking and smuggling, organ traffic, sex tourism, the loss of original culture and identity (language, customs and spiritual practices), criminalization and assassination of leaders and defenders of the territory. Behind all this are dominant economic and political interests, with the complicity of some government officials and some indigenous authorities. The victims are the most vulnerable: children, youth, women and our sister mother earth.[39]

From Sen's perspective, the focus remains on what human beings are able to do and be, such as the ability of indigenous people in the Amazon to avoid an easily preventable death, eat food from the forests, drink water from the rivers, and express their cultures. An integral human development perspective extends this to an evaluation of what is happening to the earth and also extends the evaluation of environmental degradation to an analysis about its possible causes, such as powerful economic and political interests, corruption, and lack of love and care towards nature and people. Policies and government and international action have to change, but, from an integral human development perspective, it is not only policies that need to change, 'it is we human beings above all who have to change' (LS 220), and change so that our lives reflect more that openness to love and friendship with others and nature, that orientation to 'love in truth'.

Broadening the evaluation of states of affairs: integrating oneself

Sen's capability approach broadened the evaluation space of development beyond income to include considerations about the kinds of lives people live and what they were able to be and do. Integral human development broadens it further to include considerations about what it called the 'interior dimension' (SRS 29), that is, the extent to which our very selves are open to what is happening to the lives of others and to the earth, the extent to which our lives and decisions express love for others and the earth.

Populorum Progressio already talked of every human person's self-fulfilment as bound up with the development of human society as a whole (PP 14–17), for 'we are the heirs of earlier generations, and we reap benefits from the efforts of our contemporaries' (PP 17), and future generations will inherit the earth and society we will have bequeathed them. *Sollicitudo Rei Socialis* takes this argument further by stressing the need for 'a change of behaviour or mentality or mode of existence' (SRS 38), for development does not only have a socio-economic dimension but also a moral dimension. Overcoming the socio-economic obstacles to the development of each person is also about 'inner growth' or 'inner transformation' (SRS 38), a journey where one grows and deepens love in one's relationship to self, neighbour, including distant ones, and nature. *Laudato Si'* talks of a 'change of heart' (LS 218).

This emphasis on inner growth and change at the personal level, of turning away from habits and actions which harm others and nature, is not unique to religious traditions. Interestingly, the Intergovernmental Panel on Climate Change (IPCC (2014: 29)) made a similar argument about personal and structural responses to climate change being both essential and mutually reinforcing. This integration of the self as a subject of development and growth at the moral level is also increasingly talked about in development studies. The move to decolonize is leading to greater self-reflexivity and critical examining of one's own position of power and privilege (Schöneberg 2019), and of one's own contribution to the problems of inequality, poverty, and environmental degradation.

In a plenary lecture at the UK Development Studies Association conference on leadership for global challenges, Batliwala (2020) argued for the integration of the psychic level into the global challenges. In addition to change in ideas and how we relate to each other and the planet, she contends that a similar attention needs to be paid to our inner selves, our internal harmony and emotional world, and that there can be no divide between personal and social transformation. As she expressed it succinctly, 'We are ready to fix the world, but not to question our own internalized sense of power and privilege'; 'new leaders are people who have to be ready to work on themselves and recognize themselves as sites of change'.[40] In other words, development practice is something that happens not only 'out there' in the so-called developing world but also in our very selves, our personal lives, and the organizations in which we work – for example, an organization which works on addressing gender inequality has to examine how it itself embeds patriarchal attitudes and treats women.

Concluding remarks

This chapter has discussed how integrating a spiritual dimension into development, in the sense of openness to the values of love and friendship, could extend further the concept and meaning of development derived from Sen's capability approach. This could be by, among other things, integrating concerns for the earth and the whole web of life into concerns for those who live in poverty and making oneself the subject of development and inner transformation. This integral human development perspective has implications for the SDGs. Not only do they have to be addressed holistically – for example, addressing poverty in all its dimensions cannot be separated from nurturing life in water and on land – but they also have to be addressed through a critical self-reflection about our own place and situation of power and privilege in economic, social, and political systems, and about our responsibility in causing social and environmental degradation. This makes an integral human development framework more prescriptive than Sen's. Both function as conceptual frameworks for a range of evaluative exercises, but integral human development links these evaluative exercises to a vision of what states of affairs are to reflect, a vision of harmonious relations between people and nature, or what Pope Francis called in his post-synodal apostolic exhortation after the Amazon Synod, *Querida Amazonia* (QA), a kind of 'personal, familial, communal and cosmic harmony' (QA 71).

Given this tying of the evaluative exercise to a certain overall normative vision, an integral human development perspective makes a stronger denunciation of situations which contrast with this vision. Within Sen's capability approach, there is an implicit moral evaluation that situations in which, for example, such as India in the late 1990s, half a country's children are malnourished or a large share of the population does not have access to a toilet, reflect indifference from those in policy decision-making processes to what happens to the life of the vulnerable (Drèze and Sen 2013). An integral human development approach expresses a more pronounced value judgement on such states of affairs. In his apostolic exhortation *Evangelii Gaudium* (EG), Pope Francis talks of rejecting an 'economy that kills', of saying 'No to an economy of exclusion', 'No to the new idolatry of money', 'No to a financial system which rules rather than serves', 'No to the inequality which spawns violence' (EG 53–60).

Both perspectives see markets as exchange mechanisms, but when such exchange mechanisms lead to human exploitation, to profits taking priority over concerns for human dignity and care for the earth, Sen's perspective limits itself to evaluating the impact of lack of market regulation on the lives of peoples. It would then submit this information to 'public reasoning' to discuss whether remedial action needs to take place and which action best to take. But as such, it does not prescribe stronger market regulations beyond pointing out the effects of market liberalization on people's lives. It leaves it to processes of public reasoning to judge the situation and act if need be (cf. Chapter 3). For example, it would evaluate the impact of the lack of regulation of agribusiness activities and of the use of pesticides on the health and lives of children who live close to soya fields; it would evaluate the impact of the lack of regulation of extractive industries, or the impact of policies incentivizing the extraction and export of natural resources, on the lives of those who live near the extractive sites. An integral human development perspective goes, however, further than mere evaluation when the lack of regulation and the search for quick profits undermine the lives of people and of ecosystems. As the bishop in charge of the archdiocese that includes one of the world's most contaminated cities, La Oroya evaluated the health situation of its residents: 'It is the money which commands.'[41] Pope Francis similarly evaluated the current situation of the Amazon rainforest and of its inhabitants:

> The businesses, national or international, which harm the Amazon and fail to respect the right of the original peoples to the land and its

boundaries, and to self-determination and prior consent, should be called for what they are: injustice and crime. When certain businesses out for quick profit appropriate lands and end up privatizing even potable water, or when local authorities give free access to the timber companies, mining or oil projects, and other businesses that raze the forests and pollute the environment, economic relationships are unduly altered and become an instrument of death.

(QA 14)

As Sachs (2017) has argued, in relation to *Laudato Si'* and the SDGs, the Catholic social tradition provides a deeper interrogation of processes of social change and a discussion of the root causes of social and environmental degradation, which it situates in a misuse of human freedom, a freedom which has been used to harm the environment instead of caring for it, a freedom that has been used to be indifferent to what is happening to vulnerable people and to the earth and choose financial gains instead.

In bringing Sen's capability approach to development in dialogue with the Catholic social tradition and its conception of development, this chapter has focused on contributions from the latter to the former. However, like any dialogue between two equal partners, the conversation can be mutually transformative for both. Sen's capability approach, and its open-ended nature and indeterminacy, and its focus on evaluation of states of affairs rather than diagnosis, could also bring some significant contributions to the Catholic social tradition, especially with regard to gender equality.

A paradox of the Catholic social tradition is, on the one hand, its teaching on human dignity and equal moral worth of each human person, and, on the other hand, its lack of attention to gender inequality. Although *Laudato Si'* has adopted gender inclusive language unlike in previous papal documents, it makes no mention of the fact that women disproportionally suffer from environmental degradation and that women are often at the forefront of care for our common home (Cahill 2018). In addition, the latest encyclical is titled in a way which ignores women (*Fratelli Tutti – To All Brothers*), though it adopts inclusive language throughout its text. It is beyond the scope of this book to engage in a discussion on how the position of the Catholic Church on the equal dignity of women and men, whatever their sexual orientation, is currently being debated and evolving (Beattie 2020; Bracke and Paternotte 2016). But one can highlight that the Catholic social tradition is far from being static and homogenous. It is in development, responding to the historical context and reflecting on the current reality of societies. Its thinking on the concept of development started in the historical context of decolonization. It has evolved to integrate a preferential option for the poor following contributions from theological reflections on the social reality of poverty and inequality, and to integrate care for the earth follow-ing contributions from theological reflection on the reality of environmental degradation. The Pope may be the signatory of an encyclical which shapes the Catholic social tradition, but it is the work of a large group of people, and some voices may be louder than others, or listened to more than others.

The Catholic Church, like any other institution, whether religious or not, is not homogenous and is not immune to abuses of power, money, and cor-ruption, or, of course, to patriarchy and sexism. Although religious leaders may make decisions through what is called in religious language 'discern-ment', this does not eliminate politics and power dynamics at play in any human relationships.[42] Sen's capability approach to development, with its focus on women's agency and gender justice and closer attention to every member being able to participate in matters that affect her life, could con-tribute to bringing the concerns of marginalized women to the core of the Catholic social tradition. The Church's own writings on solidarity and how we are to live in relation to others and nature may help in that regard, to which the next chapter turns.

Notes

1 The term 'capability' is also linked to Sen's works on poverty and famines (Sen 1981), in which he saw poverty as an entitlement failure, that is, a lack of com-mand over a bundle of commodities due to institutional factors. For a critical discussion on Sen's entitlement approach, see Devereux (2001). For a compari-son between his entitlement and capability approaches, see Reddy and Daoud (2020).

2 In 2004, a dedicated academic association, the Human Development and Capa-bility Association, was formed to support research around the ideas of the capa-bility approach; see https://hd-ca.org.

3 For an overview of Amartya Sen and Nussbaum's works on religion, see Deneulin and Zampini-Davies (2020).

4 A lot has been written on the distinction between functionings and capabilities; see Robeyns (2017) and Wolff and De-Shalit (2013) for introductory critical discussions.

5 A question-and-answer session after a public lecture given by Amartya Sen for the Oxford Poverty and Human Development Initiative in Oxford (year not remembered by the author).

6 Since 2016, the *Human Development Reports* have moved from translating 'capabilities' as 'choices' to using the full conceptual apparatus of functionings-capabilities-agency (UNDP 2016: 2).

7 The French intellectual Simone Weil took leave from her work in education as philosopher to take employment as a factory worker out of solidarity with fac-tory workers. For an account of Weil's life, see Plant (2007).

8 The civil society organization Global Witness reported 212 killings world-wide in 2019 for opposing environmental destruction and 33 deaths in the Amazon region. See www.globalwitness.org/en/press-releases/global-witness-

records-the-highest-number-of-land-and-environmental-activists-murdered-in-one-year-with-the-link-to-accelerating-climate-change-of-increasing-concern/, accessed 6 January 2021.

9 The words in inverted commas are Sen's own during a public lecture for the launch of *Collective Choice and Social Welfare*, 18 January 2017, Oxford.

10 Ezquerro-Cañete (2016) also talks of peasants in Paraguay appearing to 'choose' to sell their land to agribusinesses, but they have little choice of not doing so when their land is being poisoned by air-sprayed pesticide in neighbouring soy plantations and unfit for subsistence food cultivation.

11 The global Multidimensional Poverty Index (MPI) has included a dimension of access to water and housing quality; see www.ophi.org.uk.

12 Her ten central human capabilities are (Nussbaum 2000: 77–78, 2011: 33–34) to live a life of normal length; to have bodily health; to have bodily integrity; to think and reason (such as guarantees of freedom of expression); to express emotions; to engage in critical reflection about the planning of one's life; to engage in social interaction and have the social bases of self-respect; to live with concern for the natural environment; to laugh and play; to control one's environment (such as participation in choices that govern one's life and work).

13 The questions used to develop the index are: 'How spiritual do you consider yourself?'; 'Do you consider Karma in the course of your daily life?'; 'How often do you recite prayers?; 'How often do you meditate?' (Ura et al. 2012: 116).

14 See paragraph 33 of *Laudato Si'*: 'It is not enough, however, to think of different species merely as potential "resources" to be exploited, while overlooking the fact that they have value in themselves. Each year sees the disappearance of thousands of plant and animal species which we will never know. . . . . Because of us, thousands of species will no longer give glory to God by their very existence, nor convey their message to us. We have no such right.'

15 See www.hdr.undp.org/en/data, accessed 6 January 2021.

16 For discussions on poverty from a capability perspective, see, among others, Alkire et al. (2015), Alkire (2020) and Wolff (2020). See also Sen (1985c), where he discusses poverty as a failure to achieve certain minimum capabilities.

17 For how the Index is calculated, see https://ophi.org.uk/publications/mpi-methodological-notes/. See also www.hdr.undp.org/en/2019-MPI, accessed 6 January 2021.

18 See https://ophi.org.uk/global-mpi-report-2020, accessed 6 January 2021.

19 See https://mppn.org/multidimensional-poverty-profile-in-palestine, accessed 6 January 2021.

20 See https://mppn.org/paises_participantes/el-salvador, accessed 6 January 2021.

21 An Oxfam report has, for example, estimated that, between 2005 and 2010, the mining companies in Colombia paid the government annually USD 456 million in taxes but that they received in return USD 925 million in fiscal exemptions (Oxfam International 2015).

22 For how climate change disproportionately affects poor and marginalized communities, see, for example, Alston (2019), UNDP (2019), Islam and Winkel (2017).

23 For the historical background of *Populorum Progressio* and the influence of Joseph-Louis Lebret, see Catta (2015) and Rapela Heidt (2017). See also the Special Issue on 'Louis Joseph Lebret and the development of peoples', *Journal of Global Ethics,* edited by Des Gasper and Lori Keleher, forthcoming in 2021.

24 See www.humandevelopment.va/en/il-dicastero/motu-proprio.html, accessed 6 January 2021.
25 Paragraph 19 of the *Compendium of the Social Doctrine of the Church* (PCJP 2005), quoted on the Dicastery's website; see www.humandevelopment.va/en/sviluppo-umano-integrale/fede-e-sviluppo-integrale.html, accessed 6 January 2021.
26 For the secondary literature on integral human development, see, among others, Bertina (2013), Catta (2015, 2019), Keleher (2018), Kraemer (1998), Pfeil (2018), Pope (2019).
27 See Townsend (2017), '5.3.4 Henri de Lubac and Louis-Joseph Lebret', at https://virtualplater.org.uk/module-b/b-unit-1-contents/5-3populorum-progressio/5-3-4-henri-de-lubac-and-louis-joseph-lebret/ (accessed 6 January 2021), quoting Avery Dulles SJ, 'Henri de Lubac: In Appreciation', America, 28 Sept. 1991. For a summary of de Lubac's works, see Kerr (2006).
28 www.vatican.va/content/francesco/en/speeches/2017/april/documents/papa-francesco_20170404_convegno-populorum-progressio.html, accessed 6 January 2021.
29 Ibid.
30 See Dorr (2016) for an analysis of how the key documents of the Catholic social tradition are a response to changing socio-economic contexts.
31 For a discussion on the relationship between spirituality and religion, see Schneiders (2003).
32 See editorial of *The Lancet*, 'We need to talk about meat', volume 392, issue 10161, P2237, 24 November 2018, https://doi.org/10.1016/S0140-6736(18)32971-4.
33 See, for example, the World Health Organization's work on bringing more awareness of the health consequences of electronic waste; www.who.int/activities/raising-awareness-on-e-waste-and-children-s-health, accessed 6 January 2021.
34 For discussions on the relation between human dignity and human rights, and implications for development, see Carozza and Sedmak (2020), Clark (2014), and Gilabert (2018); for a discussion on the relation between the capability approach and human rights, see Elson, Fukuda-Parr and Vizard (2012), Vizard (2006, 2020), and Sen (2005); see also Nussbaum (2000, 2011) for an anchoring of the capability approach into a notion of human dignity.
35 *Gaudium et Spes,* Pastoral Constitution on the Church in the Modern World, par. 1, www.vatican.va/archive/hist_councils/ii_vatican_council/documents/vat-ii_cons_19651207_gaudium-et-spes_en.html, accessed 6 January 2021.
36 The expression was coined in 1979 at the third Latin American Bishops' Conference in Puebla, Mexico. The previous conference in 1968 at Medellín, Colombia, already affirmed that the defence of the poor was the essential task of evangelization of the Latin American Church. For the concluding documents of the two conferences (in Spanish), see, respectively, www.celam.org/doc_conferencias/Documento_Conclusivo_Medellin.pdf; https://celam.org/documentos/Documento_Conclusivo_Puebla.pdf
37 For discussions on the preferential option for the poor, see, among others, Groody, Gutierrez and Aylwin (2014), Gutierrez (2013), Schlag (2019).
38 *Laudato Si'* distinguishes between nature and creation: the latter as seeing nature as a gift and the former as something that can be studied (LS 76).
39 Paragraph 10, final document of the Amazon Synod, October 2019, www.sinodoamazonico.va/content/sinodoamazonico/en/documents/final-document-

of-the-amazon-synod.html, accessed 6 January 2021. For a report on the impact of logging, extractive activities, and infrastructure megaprojects on the Amazon region, see Bebbington et al. (2019).
40 Author's notes from Batliwala's lecture.
41 Bishop Pedro Barreto, comment made at a conference on Religions and the Sustainable Development Goals, 6–8 March 2019, Vatican City. His words were in Spanish 'Es el dinero que manda' (author's conference notes).
42 For a discussion on how discernment is at the core of Pope Francis's leadership and decision-making, see Ivereigh (2019). For a political analysis of power dynamics in the Vatican, see Reese (1996).

References

Agarwal, Bina, Jane Humphries and Ingrid Robeyns (eds). 2008. *Amartya Sen's Work and Ideas: A Gender Perspective*, Abingdon: Routledge.

Alkire, Sabina. 2002. *Valuing Freedoms*, Oxford: Oxford University Press.

———. 2020. "The Research Agenda on Multidimensional Poverty Measurement," in Enrica Chiappero-Martinetti, Siddiqur Osmani and Mozaffar Qizilbash (eds), *Cambridge Handbook of the Capability Approach*, Cambridge: Cambridge University Press, pp. 417–36, https://doi.org/10.1017/9781316335741.024.

Alkire, Sabina et al. 2015. *Multidimensional Poverty Measurement and Analysis*, Oxford: Oxford University Press, https://multidimensionalpoverty.org.

Alston, Phillip. 2019. *Climate Change and Poverty: Report of the Special Rapporteur on Extreme Poverty and Human Rights*, Geneva: Human Rights Council, https://digitallibrary.un.org/record/3810720.

Anand, Paul et al. 2020. *Multidimensional Perspectives on Inequality: Conceptual and Empirical Challenges*, Luxembourg: European Union, https://ec.europa.eu/jrc/en/publication/eur-scientific-and-technical-research-reports/multidimensional-perspectives-inequality-conceptual-and-empirical-challenges.

Bagchi, Amiya. 2000. "Review: Freedom and Development as End of Alienation?" *Economic and Political Weekly* 35(50): 4408–20, www.jstor.org/stable/4410058?seq=1.

Batliwala, Srilatha. 2020. "Rethinking Leadership for Global Challenges," Development Studies Association Conference, Forthcoming in Oxford Development Studies, Video Lecture at, www.devstud.org.uk/conference/conference-2020/plenaries/.

Baujard, Antoinette and Muriel Gilardone. 2017. "Sen Is Not a Capability Theorist," *Journal of Economic Methodology* 24(1): 1–19, https://doi.org/10.1080/1350178X.2016.1257821.

Beattie, Tina. 2020. "Human Dignity and Rights in the Context of Gender and the Sacramental Priesthood," *Interdisciplinary Journal for Religion and Transformation in Contemporary Society* 6(1): 140–57, https://doi.org/10.30965/23642807-00601009.

Bebbington, Denise et al. 2019. *Extractive Industry and Infrastructure in the Amazon*, www.climateandlandusealliance.org/reports/impacts-of-extractive-industry-and-infrastructure-on-forests/.

Bertina, Ludovic. 2013. "The Catholic Doctrine of 'Integral Human Development' and its Influence on the International Development Community," *Revue Internationale de Politique de Développement* 1(4): 115–27, https://doi.org/10.4000/poldev.1402.

Boff, Leonardo. 1997. *Cry of the Earth, Cry of the Poor*, Maryknoll, NY: Orbis Books.

Bracke, Sarah and David Paternotte. 2016. "Unpacking the Sin of Gender," *Religion and Gender* 6(2): 143–54, doi: 10.18352/rg.10167.

Cahill, Lisa Sowle. 2018. "The Environment, the Common Good, and Women's Participation," in Celia Deane-Drummond and Rebecca Artinian-Kaiser (eds), *Theology and Ecology Across the Disciplines: On Care for our Common Home*, London: T&T Clark, pp. 135–48.

Carozza, Paolo and Clemens Sedmak (eds). 2020. *The Practice of Human Development and Dignity*, Notre Dame, Indiana: University of Notre Dame Press.

Catta, Grégoire. 2015. "God For Us' in the Challenge of Integral Human Development: Theology in Post-Vatican II Catholic Social Teaching," PhD, Massachusetts: Boston College.

———. 2019. *Catholic Social Teaching as Theology*, Mahwah, NJ: Paulist Press.

Chiappero-Martinetti, Enrica, Siddiq Osmani and Mozaffar Qizilbash (eds). 2020. *The Cambridge Handbook of the Capability Approach*, Cambridge: Cambridge University Press.

Clark, Meghan. 2014. *The Vision of Catholic Social Thought*, Minneapolis: Fortress Press.

Comim, Flavio, Sabina Alkire and Mozaffar Qizilbash (eds). 2008. *The Capability Approach: Concepts, Measures and Applications*, Cambridge: Cambridge University Press.

Corbridge, Stuart. 2002. "Development as Freedom: The Spaces of Amartya Sen," *Progress in Development Studies* 2(3): 183–217, https://doi.org/10.1191/1464993402ps037ra.

Correia, Joel. 2019. "Soy States: Resource Politics, Violent Environments and Soybean Territorialization in Paraguay," *The Journal of Peasant Studies* 46(2): 316–36, https://doi.org/10.1080/03066150.2017.1384726.

Dean, Hartley. 2009. "Critiquing Capabilities: The Distractions of a Beguiling Concept," *Critical Social Policy* 29(2): 261–73, https://doi.org/10.1177/0261018308101629.

Deneulin, Séverine and Augusto Zampini-Davies. 2020. "Religion and the Capability Approach," in Enrica Chiappero-Martinetti, Siddiqur Osmani and Mozaffar Qizilbash (eds), *Cambridge Handbook of the Capability Approach*, Cambridge: Cambridge University Press, pp. 689–708, https://doi.org/10.1017/9781316335741.039.

Devereux, Stephen. 2001. "Sen's Entitlement Approach: Critiques and counter-critiques," *Oxford Development Studies* 29(3): 245–63, https://doi.org/10.1080/13600810120088859.

Dorr, Donal. 2016. *Option for the Poor and for the Earth*, Revised edition, Maryknoll, NY: Orbis.

Drèze, Jean and Amartya Sen. 2013. *An Uncertain Glory: India and its Contradictions*, London: Allen Lane.

Elson, Diane, Sakiko Fukuda-Parr and Polly Vizard (eds). 2012. *Human Rights and the Capabilities Approach: An Interdisciplinary Dialogue*, London: Routledge.

Ezquerro-Cañete, Arturo. 2016. "Poisoned, Dispossessed and Excluded: A Critique of the Neoliberal Soy Regime in Paraguay," *Journal of Agrarian Change* 16(4): 702–11, https://doi.org/10.1111/joac.12164.

Fischer, Andrew. 2018. *Poverty as Ideology: Rescuing Social Justice from Global Development Agendas*, London: Zed Books.

Frediani, Alex. 2015. "Space and Capabilities: Approaching Informal Settlements," in C. Lemanski and C. Marx (eds), *The City in Urban Poverty*, Cambridge: Cambridge University Press, pp. 64–84.

Gilabert, Pablo. 2018. *Human Dignity and Human Rights*, Oxford: Oxford University Press.

Gutierrez, Gustavo. 2013. "The Option for the Poor Arises from Faith in Christ," in M. Griffin and J. Weiss Block (eds), *In the Company of the Poor: Conversations with Paul Farmer and Gustavo Gutierrez*, Maryknoll, NY: Orbis Books, pp. 147–60.

Groody, David, Gustavo Gutiérrez and José Aylwin (eds). 2014. *The Preferential Option for the Poor beyond Theology*, Notre Dame, Indiana: University of Notre Dame Press.

Hall, David. 2019. "New Zealand's Living Standards Framework: What Might Amartya Sen Say?" *Policy Quarterly* 15(1), 38–45, https://openrepository.aut. ac.nz/handle/10292/13098.

Hamilton, Lawrence. 2019. *Amartya Sen*, Cambridge: Polity Press.

Heinrich, Geoff et al. 2008. *A User's Guide to Integral Human Development*, Baltimore: Catholic Relief Services, www.crs.org/sites/default/files/tools-research/users-guide-to-integral-human-development.pdf.

IPCC (Intergovernmental Panel on Climate Change). 2014. *Fifth Assessment Report: Summary for Policy-Makers*, www.ipcc.ch/pdf/assessment-report/ar5/syr/AR5_SYR_FINAL_SPM.pdf.

Islam, Nazrul and John Winkel. 2017. *Climate Change and Social Inequality*, DESA Working Paper No. 152, United Nations, Department of Economic & Social Affairs, www.un.org/esa/desa/papers/2017/wp152_2017.pdf.

Ivereigh, Austen. 2019. *Wounded Shepherd: Pope Francis and his Struggle to Convert the Catholic Church*, New York: Henry Holt and Company.

Keleher, Lori. 2018. "Integral Human Development," in J. Dydryk and L. Keleher (eds), *Handbook of Development Ethics*, London: Routledge, pp. 29–34.

Kerr, Fergus. 2006. *Twentieth-Century Catholic Theologians*, Oxford: Wiley-Blackwell.

Kraemer, Barbara. 1998. "Development: Principles for Integral Human Development in *Sollicitudo Rei Socialis*," *International Journal of Social Economics* 25(11/12): 1727–38, https://doi.org/10.1108/03068299810233394.

McGrath, Simon. 2018. *Education and Development*, Abingdon: Routledge.

Mitchell, Ann and Jimena Maccio. 2018. "Same City, Worlds Apart: Multidimensional Poverty and Residential Segregation in Buenos Aires," *Anales de la Asociación Argentina de Economia Politica*, https://repositorio.uca.edu.ar/bitstream/123456789/9376/1/same-city-worlds-apart.pdf.

Mitra, Sophie. 2016. "The Capability Approach and Disability," *Journal of Disability Policy Studies* 16(4): 236–47, https://doi.org/10.1177/104420730601600 40501.

Nussbaum, Martha. 2000. *Women and Human Development*, Cambridge: Cambridge University Press.

———. 2011. *Creating Capabilities: The Human Development Project*, Cambridge, MA: Harvard University Press.

OECD. 2013. *How's Life? 2013: Measuring Well-being*, Paris: OECD, www.oecd.org/sdd/3013071e.pdf.

Oxfam International. 2015. *Privilegios que Niegan Derechos. Desigualdad Extrema y Secuestro de la Democracia en América Latina y el Caribe*, Oxfam International, www.oxfam.org/es/informes/privilegios-que-niegan-derechos.

Pfeil, Margaret. 2018. "Fifty Years after *Populorum Progressio*: Understanding Integral Human Development in the Light of Integral Ecology," *Journal of Catholic Social Thought* 15(1): 5–17, https://doi.org/10.5840/jcathsoc20181512.

Plant, Stephen. 2007. *The SPCK Introduction to Simone Weil*, London: SPCK.

Pontifical Council for Justice and Peace (PCJP). 2005. *Compendium of the Social Doctrine of the Church*, Rome. www.vatican.va/roman_curia/pontifical_councils/justpeace/documents/rc_pc_justpeace_doc_20060526_compendio-dott-soc_en.html.

Pope, Stephen. 2019. "Integral Human Development: From Paternalism to Accompaniment," *Theological Studies* 80(1): 123–47, https://doi.org/10.1177/0040563918819798.

Rapela Heidt, Mari. 2017. "Development, Nations, and 'The Signs of the Times'," *Journal of Moral Theology* 6(1): 1–20, https://jmt.scholastichq.com/article/11330-development-nations-and-the-signs-of-the-times-the-historical-context-of-populorum-progressio.

Reddy, Sanjay and Adel Daoud. 2020. "Entitlements and Capabilities," in Enrica Chiappero-Martinetti, Siddiqur Osmani and Mozaffar Qizilbash (eds), *Cambridge Handbook of the Capability Approach*, Cambridge: Cambridge University Press, pp. 677–85, doi: 10.1017/9781316335741.038.

Reese, Thomas. 1996. *Inside the Vatican: The Politics and Organization of the Catholic Church*, Cambridge, MA: Harvard University Press.

Robeyns, Ingrid. 2017. *Wellbeing, Freedom and Social Justice: The Capability Approach Re-Examined*, Cambridge: Open Book Publishers, www.openbookpublishers.com/product/682.

———. 2019. "What, if Anything, Is Wrong with Extreme Wealth?" *Journal of Human Development and Capabilities* 20(3): 251–66, https://doi.org/10.1080/19452829.2019.1633734.

Sachs, Wolfgang. 2017. "The Sustainable Development Goals and Laudato Si': Varieties of Post-Development?" *Third World Quarterly* 38(12): 2573–87.

Schlag, Martin. 2019. "The Preferential Option for the Poor and Catholic Social Teaching," in G. V. Bradley and E. C. Brugger (eds), *Catholic Social Teaching: A Volume of Scholarly Essays*, Cambridge: Cambridge University Press, pp. 468–82.

Schneiders, Sandra. 2003. "Religion vs. Spirituality: A Contemporary Conundrum," *Spiritus: A Journal of Christian Spirituality* 3(2): 163–85, https://scholarcom mons.scu.edu/cgi/viewcontent.cgi?article=1087&context=jst.

Schöneberg, Julia. 2019. "Imagining Postcolonial Development Studies: Reflection on Positionality and Research Practices," in Elisabetta Basile, Isa Baud, Tina Kontinen and Susanne von Itter (eds), *Building Development Studies for the New Millennium*, New York: Palgrave Macmillan, pp. 97–116.

Sen, Amartya. 1970. "The Impossibility of a Paretian Liberal," *Journal of Political Economy* 78(1): 152–57, doi: 10.2307/1829633.

———. 1980. "Equality of What?" in S. McMurrin (ed), *Tanner Lectures on Human Values*, Cambridge: Cambridge University Press, pp. 197–220, https://tannerlec tures.utah.edu/_documents/a-to-z/s/sen80.pdf.

———. 1981. *Poverty and Famines: An Essay on Entitlement and Deprivation*, Oxford: Clarendon Press.

———. 1985a. *Commodities and Capabilities*, Amsterdam: North Holland.

———. 1985b. "Well-being, Agency and Freedom: The Dewey Lectures 1984," *Journal of Philosophy* 82(4): 169–221, doi: 10.2307/2026184.

———. 1985c. "A Sociological Approach to the Measurement of Poverty: A Reply to Professor Peter Townsend," *Oxford Economic Papers* 37(4): 669–76.

———. 1988. "The Concept of Development," in Ch. Hollis and T. N. Srinivasan (eds), *Handbook of Development Economics*, Volume 1, Amsterdam: Elsevier, pp. 9–26.

———. 1992. *Inequality Re-Examined*, Oxford: Clarendon Press.

———. 1999. *Development as Freedom*, Oxford: Oxford University Press.

———. 2003. "Development as Capability Expansion," in S. Fukuda-Parr and A. K. Shiva Kumar (eds), *Readings in Human Development*, Oxford: Oxford University Press, pp. 3–16.

———. 2004. "Why Should We Preserve the Spotted Owl," *London Review of Books* 26(3): 101, www.lrb.co.uk/the-paper/v26/n03/amartya-sen/why-we-should-preserve-the-spotted-owl.

———. 2005. "Human Rights and Capabilities," *Journal of Human Development* 6(2): 151–66, https://doi-org.ezproxy1.bath.ac.uk/10.1080/14649880500120491.

———. 2014. "The Contemporary Relevance of Buddha," *Ethics and International Affairs* 28(1): 15–27, https://doi.org/10.1017/S0892679414000033.

———. 2015. *The Country of First Boys*, New Delhi: Oxford University Press.

———. 2017. *Collective Choice and Social Welfare*, London: Allen Lane.

Sen, Amartya and Martha Nussbaum (eds). 1993. *The Quality of Life*, Oxford: Oxford University Press.

Seth, Suman and Maria Emma Santos. 2020. "Multidimensional Inequality and Human Development," in Enrica Chiappero-Martinetti, Siddiqur Osmani and Mozaffar Qizilbash (eds), *Cambridge Handbook of the Capability Approach*,

Cambridge: Cambridge University Press, pp. 392–416, https://doi.org/10.1017/9781316335741.023.

Svampa, Maristella. 2019. *Neo-Extractivism in Latin America*, Elements in Politics and Society in Latin America Series, Cambridge: Cambridge University Press.

Tearfund. 2016. *An Introductory Guide to the LIGHT Wheel Toolkit*, https://learn.tearfund.org/en/resources/impact_and_effectiveness/the_light_wheel/.

Terzi, Lorella. 2020. "Capability and Disability," in Enrica Chiappero-Martinetti, Siddiqur Osmani and Mozaffar Qizilbash (eds), *Cambridge Handbook of the Capability Approach*, Cambridge: Cambridge University Press, pp. 544–61, https://doi.org/10.1017/9781316335741.031.

Townsend, Nicholas. 2017. *Virtual Plater: Catholic Social Teaching Gateway, Module B: Living in a Just and Free Society*, Birmingham: Newman University, https://virtualplater.org.uk/module-b/outline-of-module-b/.

UNDP. 2016. *Human Development Report: Human Development for Everyone*, www.hdr.undp.org/sites/default/files/2016_human_development_report.pdf.

———. 2019. *Human Development Report: Beyond Income, Beyond Averages, Beyond Today: Inequalities in Human Development in the 21st Century*, www.hdr.undp.org/sites/default/files/hdr2019.pdf.

———. 2020. *Human Development Report. The Next Frontier: Human Development and the Anthropocene*, http://hdr.undp.org/.

Ura, Karma et al. 2012. *An Extensive Analysis of GNH Index*, Centre for Bhutan Studies, https://ophi.org.uk/policy/national-policy/gross-national-happiness-index/.

Valencia, Areli. 2016. *Human Rights Trade-Offs in Times of Economic Growth: The Long-Term Capability Impacts of Extractive-Led Development*, New York: Palgrave Macmillan.

Van Jaarsveld, Jessica. 2020. "Nussbaum's Capability Approach and African Environment Ethics," *Oxford Development Studies* 48(2): 135–48, https://doi.org/10.1080/13600818.2020.1759037.

Venkatapuram, Sridhar. 2011. *Health Justice: An Argument from the Capabilities Approach*, Cambridge: Polity Press.

Vizard, Polly. 2006. *Poverty and Human Rights: Sen's Capability Perspective Explored*, Oxford: Oxford University Press.

———. 2020. "The Capability Approach and Human Rights," in Enrica Chiappero-Martinetti, Siddiqur Osmani and Mozaffar Qizilbash (eds), *Cambridge Handbook of the Capability Approach*, Cambridge: Cambridge University Press, pp. 624–42, doi: 10.1017/9781316335741.035.

Vizard, Polly and Liz Speed. 2016. "Examining Multidimensional Inequality and Deprivation in Britain Using the Capability Approach," *Forum for Social Economics* 45(2–3): 139–69, https://doi.org/10.1080/07360932.2014.997267.

Walker, Melanie and Elaine Unterhalter (eds). 2007. *Amartya Sen's Capability Approach and Social Justice in Education*, Basingstoke: Palgrave Macmillan.

Watene, Krushil. 2016. "Valuing Nature: Māori Philosophy and the Capability Approach," *Oxford Development Studies* 44(3): 287–97, https://doi.org/10.1080/13600818.2015.1124077.

Wolff, Jonathan. 2020. "Beyond Poverty," in V. Beck, H. Hahn and R. Lepenies (eds), *Dimensions of Poverty. Philosophy and Poverty*, Volume 2, Cham: Springer, https://link.springer.com/book/10.1007/978-3-030-31711-9.

Wolff, Jonathan and Avner De-Shalit. 2013. *Disadvantage*, 2nd edition, Oxford: Oxford University Press.

2 Anthropological visions

Conceiving development as being about improving human lives inescapably raises questions about what it means to live a human life. The previous chapter addressed these questions by arguing that, for Sen's capability approach and the conception of development it undergirds, one aspect of being human is about being able to live a life one has reason to value and to be an agent, an author of one's life. While not being prescriptive about policy priorities, there is an implicit assumption that a main policy priority is to provide the conditions for each human being to live a minimally acceptable human life. The Catholic social tradition, as it has been articulated in recent years, goes further than Sen's by connecting the types of lives that humans live with how well ecosystems function, and the flourishing of human beings with that of the flourishing of the whole web of life. This chapter further explores how both Sen's capability approach and the Catholic social tradition conceive what it is to be human. As in the previous chapter, it does not aim to be an exhaustive summary of Sen's works, nor a discussion of Catholic theological anthropology. Rather, it highlights some central features of each and draws some implications for development theory and practice.

How one conceives what it is to be human, whether, for example, as a self-interested maximizer of one's own utility or whether as an interdependent carer for others and the earth, is not without practical and policy implications. A greater awareness of human interdependence with the natural world translates into different social practices and sets of regulations and policies (UNDP 2020, cf. Conclusion). At an individual level, this greater awareness can translate into practices such as stimulating biodiversity and protecting endangered species in one's garden. At a policy level, this could translate into policies that seek to combine the protection of the biodiversity of forests with economic livelihoods – in the case of Brazil, for example, it has been demonstrated that the financial gains of fostering a bio-economy in the Amazon region would be greater than the

DOI: 10.4324/9781003121534-3

gains of soya and beef production which drive deforestation (Nobre and Nobre 2019).

This chapter follows the same structure as the previous one. It starts by examining the underlying anthropological vision in Sen's capability approach to development. Each person is considered as an ultimate end and as having equal moral worth, but the human person is also considered within a complex web of relationships. The faculties of listening, speaking, interacting with others, showing empathy, taking the suffering of others as one's own, and reasoning with others about which courses of action to take are seen as core human faculties. Given its open-ended nature, the anthropological vision of Sen's capability approach can facilitate dialogue with other similarly relational anthropological visions, such as that of indigenous cosmologies. The chapter then discusses how the Catholic social tradition views what it is to be human and how it extends that of Sen's. It describes how the Catholic social tradition maintains the principle of each person as an end but puts a stronger emphasis on how well people's relationships are doing, with each other and with nature. It also goes further in connecting the socio-environmental crisis with the exercise of human freedom, which, of course, may not always be oriented to the good of others and nature. It similarly emphasizes the core human faculties of listening, interacting, empathy, and reasoning but extends listening to the non-human world and emphasizes gratitude. The chapter concludes by examining how Sen's capability approach to development could itself contribute to the Catholic social tradition with its greater focus on reasoning and on women's marginalization.

The anthropological vision of Sen's conception of development

Each individual person, in relationships, as an end

Sen's conception of development emerged from a critique of utilitarianism and its focus on the greater good for the greatest number and on its disregard for what happens in the life of each individual. A country like Peru can increase its gross domestic product through more extractive activities and redistribute some of the public revenues which arise from these activities through a public pension scheme and expansion of public services, but the lives of a few thousand people who live on land used for new mining explorations may be negatively affected, with the loss of agricultural livelihoods. From a utilitarian perspective, these negative consequences can be justified as long as the lives of other Peruvians are improved sufficiently to offset the loss. Illustrating this logic, a former president of Peru, Alan Garcia, therefore argued that 400,000 people who are opposing mining projects had no right to undermine the general good of 28 million Peruvians and that one could not let mineral-rich land idle (what he called 'the dog in the manger syndrome').[1] In contrast, from a capability approach perspective, the life of each person matters. The moral justification for harming some lives for the sake of expanding public revenues and the reach of public services is more complex than achieved from a simple utilitarian metric. Each person is regarded as an ultimate end and with equal moral worth.

This principle of each individual person as an end has been called 'ethical individualism' (Robeyns 2008, 2017), for what matters ultimately is what happens not to a group or country as a whole but to each person. Following Nussbaum (2011), Robeyns (2017) sees ethical individualism as part of treating all human beings as moral equals. Some considerable misunderstanding has been generated by the term 'ethical individualism'. Many have criticized the capability approach for being too individualistic because it focuses on each individual person as an end and not groups, ignoring the inherent social dimension of human existence.[2] This section aims at clarifying why Sen's capability approach is not individualistic and argues that its underlying anthropology is fundamentally relational.

A first ground for misinterpreting Sen's perspective for being too individualistic lies in its open-ended nature. As the previous chapter has highlighted, Sen has proposed an *approach* for thinking about questions of development and justice, and not a theory. It is from that specific approach, what he calls that specific 'line of thinking', that a certain way of conceiving what counts as 'development' or 'good social change' has emerged. A side effect of such open-endedness is vulnerability to misinterpretation. The naming of the principle of each person as an end, of every individual person as having an inalienable worth (which could be seen as akin to the principle of human dignity of the Catholic social tradition), as 'ethical individualism', has unfortunately led to the perception of the approach as excessively concerned with individuals and their freedoms.

Questioned on how he viewed the individual–society relation, Amartya Sen commented that it was a 'folly' to separate the individual from the social connections which made the person who she is, and that an individual's faculties 'to think and value are linked to his or her social existence and connections with each other'.[3] To be a human being is to interact with others (Sen 2015: 81). As he puts it in *The Idea of Justice*, it is hard 'to envision cogently how persons in society can think, choose, or act without being influenced in one way or another by the nature of the working of the world around them' (Sen 2009: 244–5).

Seeing each person as having equal moral worth does not mean that *only* what happens to the lives of individuals should be taken into account when assessing situations. Considerations about structures can also be included, such as the caste system, political systems, and cultural and social norms. For example, one can assess the situations of indigenous peoples in the Amazon region according to what each individual person can be or do, whether she is able to avoid hunger or diseases, or be in relation with the forest. Seeing each person as a moral equal does not rule out an analysis of political structures that prevent people from having a say in the decisions which affect their territories and their lives.

According to Robeyns (2017), whether one extends the evaluation space beyond individual considerations depends on the nature of the evaluative exercise, but it is not a requirement of the capability approach as such. It is optional, as far as the evaluative exercise is concerned, to analyse the structures themselves, such as how political systems function to exclude certain groups (e.g. how indigenous peoples in the Amazon are excluded from the policy decisions which affect the Amazon region), how patriarchal social norms discriminate against women (e.g. a woman not being able to study or work because her husband prevents her from doing so), or how a consumer culture is creating plastic islands in oceans that destroy ecosystems or large amounts of electronic waste which are affecting children's health (WHO 2017), or generating significant socio-environmental damage through 'fast fashion' (Niinimäki et al. 2020). In its *Human Development Reports*, the UNDP has taken the step to extend the evaluation space of development beyond individual considerations to include 'structures of living together' (UNDP 2016: 89–91),[4] such as social norms that create and maintain racism, or social norms that favour carbon-intensive and unsustainable lifestyles, and structures of inequality, such as how political systems are structured to include the voices of the most marginalized and those most affected by climate change (UNDP 2019, 2020), or the voices of future generations (Stewart 2020).

There is some ambiguity in Sen's own writings about whether the evaluation of how people's lives are doing should be limited to considerations about individual lives or whether it should include information about structures of living together and the extent to which they facilitate, or undermine, the flourishing of people (and ecosystems). In *The Idea of Justice*, Sen argues for limiting the evaluation space to individual considerations and that it is sufficient to recognize interdependence and interaction, and the ability of individuals to participate in social life: 'In valuing a person's ability to take part in the life of society, there is an implicit valuation of the life of the society itself, and that is an important enough aspect of the capability perspective' (Sen 2009: 246). However, in his writings on India co-authored with Jean Drèze, there is a departure from focusing exclusively on how individuals are doing to how they relate to each other and the way a society as a whole is structured. In *An Uncertain Glory*, Drèze and Sen (2013: 213) talk of the 'grip of inequality', of gender, caste, and class, on India's society. They emphasize that these require a full analysis that is not achieved by simply looking at the effect structures have on individual achievements, like health or educational outcomes.

In order to evaluate how people's lives are doing beyond individual considerations, some have proposed to extend the evaluation space to collective capabilities or relational capabilities.[5] As attractive as the idea of collective capabilities might be in order to highlight that humans can only flourish in relationships, the idea risks introducing a false dichotomy between individual and community. Two problems can be highlighted. First, the concept of capability implies the action of deciding or choosing. Individual human beings do indeed think and act only in relationships, but it is not the relationship as such which acts or decides. A collective decision is not detached from what individual persons decide. Costa Rica may have taken the collective decision, as a country, to become carbon neutral by 2050 and adopt a National Decarbonization Plan which both addresses social inequality and climate change,[6] but such a collective decision is not separate from how individuals, in the past and present, have taken decisions.[7] The bold policy decisions that Costa Rica's political leaders took in the 1940s to introduce a universal social security scheme have formed the background of current policy decisions to introduce a national decarbonization plan that fully incorporates social equality and human rights considerations (Araya 2020).

A second problem with the idea of collective capability is that it has come to mean whatever people can be and do as a result of collective action. In her critical review, Robeyns (2017: 116) argues that 'what makes the idea of "collective capability" plausible, is that a group or collective is needed to engage in collective action in order to reach the capability that the members of that group find valuable'. She refers to Sen (2002) pointing out in his response to his critics that, to a great extent, any capability is a 'socially dependent individual capability', that is, 'a person's capability, which that person enjoys, but for which the person is dependent on others to have that capability realised' (quoted in Robeyns 2017: 116). She concludes that

> the fundamental reason to keep and use the term 'collective capability' is that we may want to make a distinction between [a person's] capabilities that are only realisable with the help of [one or more] others, versus capabilities that require a group or collective to act in order to secure a capability for the members of that group.
>
> (Robeyns 2017: 116)

For example, the capability to eat of an 80-year-old computer-illiterate British person who is shielding from Covid-19 is a 'socially dependent individual capability' because it depends on others, such as neighbours doing the shopping for her, but the capability to eat of a 50-year-old farmer in the Amazon whose land has been contaminated by extractive industries would be a 'collective capability', as it requires a collective action to regulate the activities of extractive industries and protect his land from contamination.[8]

Speaking, listening, empathy, and reasoning

It is in a box featured in the *Human Development Report* 2013 and entitled 'What is it like to be a human being?' that Amartya Sen probably most succinctly describes the anthropological vision underpinning his conception of development. To speak, to enter into dialogue, to reason with others – these are central to what it is to be human. He uses the analogy of a person wearing an ill-fitting shoe to illustrate his argument that the abilities to speak, to express oneself, and to listen are fundamental to remedying injustice: 'Only the wearer may know where the shoe pinches, but pinch-avoiding arrangements cannot be effectively undertaken without giving voice to the people and giving them extensive opportunities for discussion' (Sen 2013: 24). As he has put it elsewhere, 'To be able to speak to each other, to hear one another, cannot but be a central capability that we human beings have great reason to value' (Sen 2015: 88).

To be able to express oneself to others and articulate the pain, or the 'pinch', that certain social and political arrangements are causing is a critical human faculty. The social protests of Black Lives Matter and #MeToo are recent illustrations in the Anglo-Saxon context of the centrality of this human faculty of expressing oneself for addressing injustice, in these cases for addressing the pain that many suffer because of abuse, humiliation, and discrimination because of skin colour or one's gender. In his 2013 *Human Development Report* box, Amartya Sen talks of the Arab Spring as an example of the policy impact of people expressing themselves:

> The political significance of such initiatives as the so-called Arab Spring, and mass movements elsewhere in the world, is matched by the epistemic importance of people expressing themselves, in dialogue with others, on what ails their lives and what injustices they want to remove.
>
> (Sen 2013: 24)

Such expression needs, however, to meet listening ears; in the Middle East the public expression of the pain of corruption and political authoritarianism has not always been met with listening ears by those in power and thus has ended in civil war in Syria.

This faculty for expressing oneself, and what ails one's life, goes beyond the directly affected. Being able to feel the pain of others, including distant ones, is another central characteristic of how Sen conceives what it is to be a human being. He talks of these 'dialogical responsibilities' as needing to 'include representing the interest of the people who are not here to express their concerns in their own voice' (Sen 2013: 24). And he continues:

> [H]uman beings do have the capacity to think about others, and their lives, and the art of responsible and accountable politics is to broaden dialogues from narrowly self-centred concerns to the broader social understanding of the importance of the needs and freedoms of people in the future as well as today.
>
> (Sen 2013: 24)

This ability to empathize with the lives of others, the ability to put oneself in the position of another person, is what Sen (2009: 414–5) sees as a core human faculty, along with the ability to reason. Speaking about the importance of reasoning and empathy in the context of famines, he writes:

> The political compulsion in a democracy to eliminate famines depends critically on the power of public reasoning in making non-victims take on the need to eradicate famines as their own commitment. Democratic institutions can be effective only if different sections of the population appreciate what is happening to others, and if the political process reflects a broader social understanding of deprivation.
>
> (Sen 2015: xxxvii)

A lack of openness to the lives of others, and especially those who suffer from deprivations and are denied the conditions to live a minimal acceptable life, has implications for public policy priorities. In their analysis of the social and political contexts of India, Drèze and Sen (2013) document how the lives of the poor are not often the subject of discussion in the media – with news about the Indian cricket team being more prominent than news about child malnutrition. They underline the importance of the marginalized to form social movements and political organizations to make their voices heard (see Chapter 3).

These faculties of relating to one another, expressing oneself, listening to others, entering into another person's life and feeling her pain, taking the removal of her pain as one's own responsibility (such as taking the removal of other people's hunger as one's own commitment), and reasoning with others about the remedial action are the foundational elements of Sen's anthropological vision. All these faculties are at play in what Sen calls 'public reasoning', that is, discussion at all levels of society, from student union debates to street protests, from academic publications to social forums to UN or other intergovernmental summits, from newspaper articles and radio programmes to parliamentary debates and elections (see Chapter 3).

Open-ended anthropological vision

Sen's capability approach is not a theory of development that might explain why some groups are marginalized and do not have access to the conditions for a minimum acceptable life. It limits itself to proposing a certain line of thinking for interpreting situations of deprivation and seeking remedial action. All it argues is the following: that when assessing how well a society is doing, one has to pay attention to the kinds of lives people are living, whether they are able to achieve a minimum set of valuable beings and doings; and that a critical ingredient for addressing situations where people's lives are not going well is public discussions, in which humans are conceived as persons-in-relation, interacting through speaking and listening, showing empathy, and reasoning together about remedial action. His conception of development may be perceived as overemphasizing freedom as both an end and a means (cf. Sen 1999), but as this chapter has sought to clarify, its underlying anthropology is much richer than simply conceiving the human person as a free agent. The focus on freedom is linked to a corresponding focus on responsibility, listening to others, showing empathy, and self-critical examination.[9]

In addition to the critique of Sen's capability approach for being too individualistic, there is the critique that it is too anthropocentric in that it focuses on assessing situations from the perspective of the kinds of lives that humans live, and not from the perspective of how other living organisms are doing. Thus, to assess the situation of the Amazon region today, the focus would be on collecting information about the kinds of lives that people in the Amazon live and not about how the Amazon rainforest, as an ecosystem, is doing and its ability to continue being a carbon sink for humanity.[10] This critique is somewhat misplaced, however, given the open-ended nature of the capability approach. Information about the kinds of lives people live is not the *only* information one should consider for assessing states of affairs. Information about people's capabilities/functionings does not exhaust the informational basis on which to make value judgements – as the Conclusion will discuss, the 2020 *Human Development Report* makes ample evaluations of how ecosystems or earth systems are doing. And it does not reject either the relevance of information about incomes, resources, or subjective feelings of happiness in some contexts.[11]

The concept of capabilities is not a winner-takes-all concept, and questions of justice and redistribution, and development, require a much richer conceptual apparatus. As Sen (2017: 358) has insisted,

> it would be misleading to see the capability approach as standing on its own as a guide to justice, since it focuses only on some specific aspects of well-being and freedom, and there are other concerns . . . that need to be brought in to get a fuller understanding of justice than can be obtained within an exclusively 'capability approach'.

Similar conclusions can be drawn with regard to its anthropological vision. The human being is viewed as a subject-in-relation and as a reasoning subject. All Sen's conception of development points out is that, when thinking about questions of justice and development, one needs to take into account the socially interactive nature of human lives and the capacity of human beings to empathize and reason with others to remedy 'what ails their lives and what injustices they want to remove' (Sen 2013: 24).

Two important underexplored aspects of Sen's anthropological vision are particularly in urgent need of further exploration for thinking about questions of development today. One concerns the interconnectedness between the flourishing of individual human beings and that of ecosystems (Capra and Luisi 2016; Capra and Jakobsen 2017; Raworth 2018; UNDP 2020); the other concerns the faculty of human beings to inflict harm on others. Work has already started on the first by bringing Sen's conception of development in dialogue with indigenous cosmologies – as the Conclusion will discuss, the 2020 *Human Development Report* rethinks the capability/human development approach in the light of this interconnectedness of all life systems, human and non-human.

In his discussion of whether the capability approach's core principle of valuing each person as an end is compatible with its other core principle of value pluralism,[12] Kramm (2020) argues that, when incorporating the values of Māori culture, the principle of valuing each person as an end cannot be sustained.[13] According to the Māori vision, to be a human being is to be in a network of relationships with others, humans and non-humans, and with human and non-human ancestors, what they call *whakapapa* or their genealogy (Kramm 2020: 2; Watene 2016; UNDP 2020: 90–1). Within *whakapapa*, a river is valued in the same way as a human being, for there is no separation between humans and non-human entities. Both rivers and humans are seen as equal givers of life with which any newborn human subject enters into relationship. Kramm therefore proposes to restrict the notion of functionings not only to humans but also to rivers, forests, oceans, and other forms of life. This would entail, he argues, shifting the principle of ethical individualism to that of 'ethical ancestoralism' to include 'everything that the Māori regard as equal partners in their relationships, including ancestors and ecosystems' (Kramm 2020: 7), and thus modifying the capability approach to create what Robeyns (2017) has called a 'hybrid version'.

Indeed, as such, Sen's capability approach with its principle of each (human) person as an end does not accommodate seeing the river as an end. It tends to see the river as instrumental to human flourishing. If a river is polluted, this will be reflected in the local people's health outcomes. Strictly speaking, then, the perspective is anthropocentric, and the focus is on what people are able to do and be, and not on how river systems function. However, seen within its context of opening up a different line of thinking, which shifts the focus from incomes or resources to what people are able to do and be, there is no reason why its informational basis for value judgements, and for assessing situations, could not be extended to include non-human systems – which is a direction the 2020 *Human Development Report* has taken (cf. Conclusion). With such inclusion of anthropological visions that see humans as part, and not separate, of the wider web of life, Sen's capability approach will probably have to outgrow itself. The approach that ensues would then no longer be called the 'capability approach' but something else.

As Krushil Watene has recently argued, Sen's capability approach creates a platform for having a conversation about values; it opens a door, but it cannot continue to hold the conversation when entering into dialogue with Māori cosmologies.[14] What it does is highlight the importance of discussion, of interaction among humans with different values and visions of what it is to be human, and of how to relate to the rest of nature.[15] Amartya Sen has opened the door for bringing questions about what it is to be human into questions about development and progress. The next section continues this conversation by bringing in another anthropological vision.

The anthropological vision of the Catholic social tradition

Each individual person, in relation with others and the earth, as an end

The Catholic social tradition has long emphasized that it is the human being who is the ultimate end of development processes and that the growth of national production and consumption is only a means towards the end of human flourishing. In words reminiscent of Sen's, the *Compendium of the Social Doctrine of the Church* affirms that

> the social order and its development must invariably work to the benefit of the human person, since the order of things is to be subordinate

to the order of persons, and not the other way around. . . . Every political, economic, social, scientific and cultural programme must be inspired by the awareness of the primacy of each human being over society.

(PCJP 2005: 132–3)

This primacy of each human being, in her own uniqueness, echoes Sen's anthropological vision. There are, however, some different points of emphasis and areas which are extended. This section highlights two: the interaction in which human beings engage is not only among humans and its anthropological vision is not limited to serving evaluation purposes, but it also serves as a framework for diagnosis and action.

While Sen's capability approach privileges the language of interaction, the Catholic social tradition privileges that of interconnectedness. That 'everything in the world is connected' is a recurrent theme in *Laudato Si'* (LS 16, 70, 91, 117, 220, 240). There are, along with others, connections among the social, economic, cultural, political, economic, and ecological dimensions (LS 101–136). Taking the example of deforestation in the Amazon, the political dimension interconnects with the economic dimension, with Bolsonaro's government stimulating agribusinesses; this economic dimension interconnects with the cultural, in the habit of daily meat consumption, which stimulates demand for beef; this cultural dimension interconnects with the ecological one, granted the indirect impact of demand for meat on land use in the Amazonian rainforest. But above all, these dimensions interconnect with how the human being is conceived in relation to the wider web of life of the universe, whether as part of it or separate from it. Like in Sen's perspective, the human being and her flourishing are the ultimate end of economic development, but the human being is conceived as intimately connected with every other form of life, whether plant or animal. For the Catholic social tradition, to be a human being is not only to interact with other humans but also to connect, to enter into communion, with others, whether human or non-human forms of life.

Pope Benedict XVI wrote in *Caritas in Veritate* of the 'book of nature' being 'one and indivisible (CV 51, LS 6), for there is no separation between the natural and human world:[16]

There is need for what might be called a human ecology, correctly understood. The deterioration of nature is in fact closely connected to the culture that shapes human coexistence. . . . Our duties towards the environment are linked to our duties towards the human person, considered in himself and in relation to others.

(CV 51)

Because of this interconnectedness with the whole web of life, humans have special responsibility to love and care: 'Because all creatures are connected, each must be cherished with love and respect, for all of us as living creatures are dependent on one another' (LS 42).

The Catholic social tradition thus takes Sen's anthropological vision a step further. Humans are not only interacting with each other and reasoning with other humans; they are also in interaction with other creatures. This extends listening to those who suffer in the non-human world. *Laudato Si'* makes it clear that 'nature cannot be regarded as something separate from ourselves or as a mere setting in which we live. We are part of nature, included in it and thus in constant interaction with it' (LS 139). This interaction between humans and non-humans also has a purpose, that of entering into communion, into harmony. *Laudato Si'* invites every person on the planet to grow in 'a loving awareness that we are not disconnected from the rest of creatures but joined in a splendid universal communion' (LS 220). The post-synodal apostolic exhortation *Querida Amazonia* talks of indigenous peoples as expressing the striving for 'good living', as a striving for 'personal, familial, communal and cosmic harmony', which 'finds expression in a communitarian approach to existence, the ability to find joy and fulfilment in an austere and simple life, and a responsible care of nature that preserves resources for future generations' (QA 71).[17]

Because each person is in relation with each other and the rest of the web of life, the good of an individual human being is indivisible from the good of all, of other human beings and ecosystems, which the Catholic social tradition calls the 'common good' (Hollenbach 2002; PCJP 2005: 164–84), with some theologians calling it the 'cosmic common good' (Scheid 2016). The Catholic social tradition conceived this interdependence as a moral category, which establishes the foundation of solidarity with and responsibility towards each other and the earth. In his encyclical *Sollicitudo Rei Socialis* published in 1987, John Paul II defined solidarity as a 'firm and persevering determination to commit oneself to the common good; that is to say to the good of all and of each individual' (SRS 38).

As everything is interdependent, the way we use our freedom has consequences for others and the whole of nature (LS 33, LS 205). Pope Francis describes interconnectedness as an invitation to 'develop a spirituality of global solidarity' (LS 240), for there is a relation between 'a sort of super development of a wasteful and consumerist kind which forms an unacceptable contrast with the ongoing situations of dehumanizing deprivation' (LS 109, CV 22). There is an interdependence between how certain people choose to exercise their freedom – to accumulate and abuse their power, to be concerned with themselves only – and the lives of others. In words that echo Sir David Attenborough's call that to address biodiversity loss 'we require more than intelligence; we require wisdom',[18] *Laudato Si'* connects wisdom, and a wise use of the power that humanity has, to the recognition of our interconnectedness and affirmation of all forms of life:

> Never has humanity had such power over itself, yet nothing ensures that it will be used wisely, particularly when we consider how it is currently being used. We need but think of the nuclear bombs dropped in the middle of the twentieth century, or the array of technology which Nazism, Communism and other totalitarian regimes have employed to kill millions of people, to say nothing of the increasingly deadly arsenal of weapons available for modern warfare.
>
> (LS 104)

In his first homily after his election, Pope Benedict XVI, sometimes dubbed in the media as the 'green pope',[19] talked of 'external deserts in the world growing, because the internal deserts have become so vast' (quoted in LS 217). There is a connection between the 'internal desert' of lack of solidarity, of concern for others who suffer from climate change, of concern for forests which disappear, and the spreading of 'external deserts'. A shaman from Greenland expressed this argument in his context as 'the Artic is warming and the ice is melting because our hearts have grown cold'.[20] More than in Sen's, the Catholic social tradition ties the exercise of human freedom to these sets of relationships and the good of all. It recognizes that the exercise of human freedom is not always for the good and that one can act, directly or indirectly, in a way which undermines relationships with each other and other forms of life on earth. At the individual level, each person can choose the lifestyle she wants; at a societal level, each society can choose which lifestyles and behaviours to discourage through regulation and taxation (e.g. taxing more air travel, banning plastic packaging, subsidizing renewable energy, and public transport). Within such an anthropological vision, however, there are certain ways of exercising human freedom which are better than others because of their consequences for others and how they express solidarity and concern for others.

More than Sen's, the anthropological vision of the Catholic social tradition recognizes the fallible nature of human life. It recognizes that human beings can exercise their freedom to enhance or undermine the lives of others. Given our interconnectedness, the actions of some in one place have consequences for the lives of others elsewhere. When these actions accumulate, they create what this tradition calls 'structures of sin'. John Paul II defined them in *Sollicitudo Rei Socialis* as

> [t]he sum total of the negative factors working against a true awareness of the universal common good. . . . [Structures of sin] are rooted in personal sin, and thus always linked to the concrete acts of individuals who introduce these structures, consolidate them and make them difficult to remove.
>
> (SRS 36)[21]

One such structure of sin that Pope Francis mentions often is that of a 'throwaway culture', a culture of overconsumption, a culture which discards what is no longer needed or whom one no longer sees as useful for society (LS 16, 22, 43). In his latest encyclical, *Fratelli Tutti*, he talks of a 'throwaway world':

> Ultimately, persons are no longer seen as a paramount value to be cared for and respected, especially when they are poor and disabled, "not yet useful" – like the unborn, or "no longer needed" – like the elderly. We have grown indifferent to all kinds of wastefulness, starting with the waste of food.
>
> (FT 18–21)

Despite this reality of wrongdoing, the possibility of change, of turning away from one's wrong, always remains a possibility, offering a 'chance for new beginning' (LS 71), opening the way to hope. The actions of past generations may have severe consequences for current generations, such as the burning of fossil fuels in the nineteenth and twentieth centuries, yet there remains always the possibility of turning away from harmful actions and beginning something new, of making different choices, of choosing to do things differently (UNDP 2020). This process of discerning how to act in a way which is not harmful to others and the environment is however a never-ending process given the ambivalence of relationships and human activities. Renewable energy has environmental costs too. Hydro-energy entails the building of dams which often carry socio-environmental conflicts in their wake.[22] The building of electric cars generates a demand for rare earth minerals, and their extraction creates significant environmental strain on local ecosystems.[23] This is why, like Sen, the Catholic social tradition sees development, or the reduction of injustices, as an ongoing circular process, but, as the next section discusses, it adds some further elements to the process.

Listening, empathy, and reasoning, earth and gift

As in Sen's perspective, it views human beings as being able to express what 'ails their lives' (Sen 2013: 24), whether through social movements, representative organizations, media, or others, and as being able to be attentive to what is happening to others' lives. It puts, however, greater emphasis on mutual listening. Such attentiveness, known as the 'seeing' stage, is the starting point for any remedial action.[24] The biblical parable of the Good Samaritan, narrated in the Gospel of Luke, Chapter 10, offers a paradigmatic illustration of this. To be fully human is to see the world with compassion and to take action to address suffering. The text narrates the story of a Priest and a Levite who saw a wounded man lying half-dead along a road and who passed by on the opposite side, as they were more preoccupied by their religious duties than being attentive to the world around them. In contrast, a Samaritan – Samaritans were seen as inferior by those to whom the parable is addressed – passed by, saw the victim, went near him, treated his wounds, lifted him onto his own animal, took him to an inn, and paid for his care. Jesus tells this parable in response to the question posed to him: 'Who is my neighbour?' – who one is responsible for and who one is commanded to love. In *The Idea of Justice*, Sen (2009: 171–2) discusses the parable to underpin his argument about responsibility and universal concern for others, and the need to transcend religious and geographical boundaries.[25]

The parable of the Samaritan features prominently in Pope Francis's latest encyclical *Fratelli Tutti*, to introduce this dynamic of attentiveness and mutual listening and to show 'how a community can be rebuilt by men and women who identify with the vulnerability of others . . . and act as neighbours, lifting up and rehabilitating the fallen for the sake of the common good' (FT 67). Like Sen's *Idea of Justice*, the encyclical urges for the need to transcend our religious and national boundaries and 'being a neighbour to another person' (FT 1, 8, 32) – in the parable, the neighbour is not only the wounded person on the road but also the one who shows mercy (FT 56). The encyclical discusses at length the importance of 'the ability to sit down and listen to others' (FT 48), of 'silence and careful listening' (FT 49), which it associates with interpersonal encounters characterized by love. It puts also greater emphasis than Sen does on this 'aspect of our common humanity', that 'we were created for a fulfilment that can only be found in love' (FT 68), 'in the sincere gift of self to others' (FT 87). Within this (theological) anthropological vision in which humans find their fulfilment in love and gift of self to others, being indifferent to suffering is dehumanizing (FT 68).

This listening and attentiveness to what happens to the world around us is not limited to the suffering of human others but extends to the non-human others (Deane-Drummond 2019b). Being human implies the faculty of listening 'to *both* the cry of the earth and of the poor' (LS 49). On the basis of the listening exercise that preceded the Amazon Synod, with more than 80,000 people from the Amazon region taking part, Pope Francis expressed in his post-synodal exhortation *Querida Amazonia* this joint cry as a 'cry that rises up to heaven' (QA 9). A shaman from the Yanomami indigenous group in Brazil talks of the environment being 'what remains of the forest and land that were hurt by their [i.e. white men] machines. The earth cannot be split apart. If we defend the entire forest [i.e. both its human and non-human residents], it will stay alive' (Kopenawa, Bruce and Dundy 2013: 396).

This listening to the voice of nature is something that Pope Francis's namesake, Saint Francis of Assisi, prophetically practised. Animals and plants and all parts of the cosmos are 'brothers and sisters all', as his Canticle of the Sun, which opens *Laudato Si'*, expresses it.[26] The encyclical talks of the need 'to become painfully aware, to dare to turn what is happening to the world into our own personal suffering and thus to discover what each of us can do about it' (LS 19). The Catholic social tradition takes the empathy of Sen's perspective further by taking the reduction of human suffering and that of ecosystems, coral reefs, and animal and plant species in danger of extinction as the commitment of all. It talks, following St Francis of Assisi, of falling in love with nature:

> Just as happens when we fall in love with someone, whenever he [Francis] would gaze at the sun, the moon or the smallest of animals, he burst into song, drawing all other creatures into his praise. He communed with all creation . . . for to him each and every creature was a sister united to him by bonds of affection.
>
> (LS 11)[27]

Laudato Si' argues that this human faculty for awe and wonder, for appreciation of beauty, is what guards us from seeing other human beings or nature as objects to be used or exploited:

> If we approach nature and the environment without this openness to awe and wonder, if we no longer speak the language of fraternity and beauty in our relationship with the world, our attitude will be that of masters, consumers, ruthless exploiters, unable to set limits on our immediate needs.
>
> (LS 11)

It links this attitude of master and exploiter to a failure to recognize all human life and nature as a gift (LS 76, 220), as something that has been entrusted to us and that will be passed on to those who come after us (LS

159). In his encyclical *Caritas in Veritate*, Pope Benedict XVI writes that 'the human being is made for gift' (CV 34), and when this capacity of gift of oneself to others and receiving others as gift is lost, there is a risk for the human being to be 'wrongly convinced that he is the sole author of himself, his life and society' (CV 34). Failure to recognize this logic of gift has consequence for the way socio-economic development is conceived and pursued. This self-sufficiency, Pope Benedict XVI continues, may lead humans to think that they can themselves bring about their own fulfilment, through their own efforts:

> The conviction that man is self-sufficient and can successfully eliminate the evil present in history by his own action alone has led him to confuse happiness and salvation with immanent forms of material prosperity and social action. Gift by its nature goes beyond merit, its rule is that of superabundance.
>
> (CV 34)

This is why, he concludes, socio-economic development needs, if it is 'to be authentically human', 'to make room for the *principle of gratuitousness* as an expression of fraternity' (CV 34, emphasis original). When we fail to recognize each human being and nature as a gift, we risk ending up abusing the gift, not using it responsibly and respecting the balance of creation (CV 48).

This view of seeing 'earth, water and air as gifts of creation that belong to everyone' (CV 51) has strong resonance with views held by indigenous communities, for whom 'land is not a commodity but rather a gift from God and from their ancestors who rest there, a sacred space with which they need to interact if they are to maintain their identity and values' (LS 146). In his conclusion of the Amazon Synod, Pope Francis talks of an 'indigenous mysticism that sees the interconnection and interdependence of the whole of creation', a 'mysticism of gratuitousness that loves life as a gift', a 'mysticism of a sacred wonder before nature and all its forms of life' (QA 73).

For the Catholic social tradition, this viewing of all life as a gift entails special responsibilities for care, which can be exercised in many ways, such as leading frugal and low-carbon lifestyles, adopting sustainable agriculture, and engaging in policy advocacy to protect biodiversity. As Chapter 3 will elaborate, in Sen's perspective as in the Catholic social tradition, processes of public reasoning are central for discerning remedial action. One of the most illustrative cases of such a process was the attention drawn to the impact of the pesticide DDT on ecosystems by Rachel Carson in 1962 in her groundbreaking book *Silent Spring*. This led to a wide public debate on human destruction of nature and contributed to the eventual banning of the pesticide in the United States of America (Lytle 2007).

To the dynamics of speaking, listening, empathy, and public reasoning, the Catholic social tradition adds one small but important feature, that of the importance of rest and contemplation which opens up space for listening and attentiveness. One has to make silence in order to be attentive and listen to the world around us:

> We tend to demean contemplative rest as something unproductive and unnecessary, but this is to do away with the very thing which is most important about work: its meaning. We are called to include in our work a dimension of receptivity and gratuity, which is quite different from mere inactivity. Rather, it is another way of working, which forms part of our very essence. It protects human action from becoming empty activism.
>
> (LS 237)

Contemplative rest, taking time to be present to the reality among us, helps to nurture the dispositions of gratitude, attentiveness, and care (Castillo 2019). It helps us to listen to the suffering of the earth and each other, and to sustain commitment to grow in solidarity, especially with those whose lives have been undermined by an ever-increasing demand for commodities to satisfy the unlimited desires and overconsumption of some.[28]

Concluding remarks

This chapter has sought to bring the anthropological visions of Amartya Sen's conception of development and the Catholic social tradition into conversation. It has highlighted some contributions that the former makes to the latter for thinking about development, such as a vision that connects the flourishing of individual human beings to that of others and the whole web of life, a greater recognition that human freedom can sometimes be misused and not directed at the common good of society and the cosmos, a stronger emphasis on listening and attentiveness to the suffering of other people and of the earth, and a consideration of nature as a gift bestowed on humans to be bequeathed as gift to others.

As highlighted in the Introduction, the Catholic social tradition is however not static. It is in constant interaction with the context to which it speaks, and its anthropological vision has evolved over the course of centuries. In *Fratelli Tutti*, Pope Francis lamented that, and questioned why, the Catholic Church had been so slow in condemning slavery as an unjust structure which violates human dignity and treats people as objects

(FT 86, 24). In *Laudato Si'*, he acknowledges that Christianity's frequent misinterpretation of the Genesis text in which God grants humans dominion over the earth has 'encouraged the unbridled exploitation of nature' and bears some responsibility in the current environmental crisis (LS 67, cf. also White 1967). But there is one major area which the Catholic social tradition continues largely to ignore in its analysis of contemporary social realities: gender inequality and women's marginalization. As Chapter 1 mentioned, *Laudato Si'* does not make any mention of the large scholarship in the social sciences which demonstrates how women disproportionately suffer from climate change.[29] Its references to the specific issues that affect women, like maternal mortality, are never mentioned. Every day, more than 800 women die globally in childbirth because of lack of proper medical attention.[30] Yet these concerns are not represented in the official documents of the Catholic social tradition (Beattie 2016). *Fratelli Tutti* may mention several times violence against women (FT 23, 24, 227) and observe that 'the organization of societies worldwide is still far from reflecting clearly that women possess the same dignity and identical rights as men. We say one thing with words, but our decisions and reality tell another story' (FT 23). Yet the Catholic social tradition falls short of according to the issue of women's marginalization the same lengthy analysis and treatment that it does to other social and economic issues. The 'technocratic paradigm' (LS 101) and the 'utilitarian mindset' (LS 210) have been widely discussed in *Laudato Si'*, but the patriarchal mindset, and its damaging effects on human lives, is yet to receive a similar discussion. The term 'gender inequality', ubiquitous in the social sciences, has so far not appeared in a papal encyclical.

As an institution, the Catholic Church still has a long journey to make in translating its words into decisions and showing by its living reality that women should indeed receive the same treatment and be shown the same respect as men. That religious brothers had a right to vote at the Amazon Synod but not religious sisters was a gross violation of the Church's own teaching (Hansen 2019). When the title of Pope Francis's latest encyclical was announced, *Fratelli Tutti* or *All Brothers*, there was a strong reaction to the lack of inclusion of 'Sisters' (*Sorelle* in Italian) in the title. The justification for the title was faithfulness to the exact words of St Francis to an all-male audience in the thirteenth century. Even if the text is gender-inclusive throughout, its title, and the way the document will be cited in different languages, ignores women's existence.

A combination of Sen's emphasis on speaking and expressing oneself, through public protests or other actions, and the Catholic social tradition emphasis on listening and attentiveness could lead to women's voices being included more in its official documents. Such a process has started with the

Amazon Synod. For the first time in the history of the Church, the papal document which summarized the Synod discussion (the post-synodal apostolic exhortation *Querida Amazonia*) did not have the last word. It is to be read in parallel with the document that summarizes the Synod discussions in which women participated.[31] The hermeneutical cycle of speaking, listening, empathy, and reasoning has been set in motion, which is forging pathways for transformation at all levels. The third and final chapter turns to this.

Notes

1 According to this idea, indigenous peoples are the 'dog in the manger'. They consider their land as a sacred inheritance from their ancestors to be passed on to future generations and therefore choose not to exploit it, thus preventing the entire country from taking advantage of natural resources in order to generate economic growth. For further details on the discourse of the 'dog in the manger' and its social implications, see Larsen (2019).

2 See, among others, Stewart and Deneulin (2002), Stewart (2005), Deneulin (2008), Ibrahim (2020). See Robeyns (2017: 115–18) for a summary of the critiques and counter-critiques.

3 Amartya Sen, 'Connecting Capabilities: Amartya Sen in conversation with Elaine Unterhalter', Recorded interview for the International Conference of the Human Development and Capability Association, 9–11 September 2019, University of London. See www.hd-ca.org (member access only).

4 The term 'structures of living together' is taken from Paul Ricoeur's ethics *Oneself as Another*; see Deneulin (2008). Paul Ricoeur's original definition refers to the notion of institution: 'By institution, we understand the structure of living together as this belongs to a historical community, a structure irreducible to interpersonal relations and yet bound up with these' (Ricoeur 1992: 194).

5 See Ibrahim (2020) for a summary of the literature on collective capabilities and Giraud, L'Huillier and Renouard (2018) for the design of relational capabilities indices to complement indices of individual functionings.

6 Costa Rica is one of the countries that has the best performance in addressing both social and environmental imbalances in the new Planetary Pressures–Adjusted Human Development Index (UNDP 2020, cf. Conclusion).

7 I have referred to this as 'socio-historical agency' to emphasize that any decision is always embedded in a social and historical context which makes certain decisions possible and others not. The fact that Costa Rica had initiated public universal primary education in the 1880s (enabling social mixing between different income groups), introduced a social security system in the early 1940s, and abolished its army was the result of the decisions of key individuals which would not have been possible in another historical context (Deneulin 2006, 2008).

8 For a discussion of 'dispossession by contamination' in the Amazon, see, among others, Leifsen (2017).

9 See Gasper and van Staveren (2003) for a discussion on how Sen's underlying anthropology can be enriched by insights from feminist economics about the

importance of caring for others. See Deneulin (2014: chapter 3) for how freedom is linked to responsibility in Sen's works.
10 According to a report by the Brazilian National Institute for Space Research led
by Luciana Gatti and Antonio Nobre, the Amazon has reached in 2020 a tipping
point and a fifth of the forest is now a net carbon emitter; see www.bbc.co.uk/
news/science-environment-51464694, accessed 9 January 2021. See also Lovejoy and Nobre (2018).
11 See Walker (2020) on the importance of resources and incomes in the capabilities of lower-income students in South Africa to pursue higher education.
12 See Robeyns (2017) for the core principles of the capability approach, which,
she argues, any application or theory based on the approach has to respect.
13 Kramm (2020) puts forward this argument in the context of the Whanganui
River in Aotearoa, New Zealand, which was ascribed the legal status of a person
in 2017.
14 Personal communication at the Human Development and Capability Association
Conference 'New Horizons: Sustainability and Justice', 30 June–2 July 2020,
Auckland, New Zealand.
15 A similar argument can be made to extending the capability approach to ubuntu-
ethic. In contrast to what Hoffmann and Metz (2017) have argued, it is not a
question whether the focus in Sen's works on individual capabilities and individual agency is compatible or not, or can be reconciled, with more community-
focused visions, but how it can be extended to include an additional focus on
ecosystems and relationships.
16 Christian theological ethics takes as its basis that humans are made in the image
of God, following the account of the book of Genesis in the Bible. This however
does not mean that humans are separate from nature; they share their createdness
with the whole of creation. This entails that human flourishing as the ultimate
purpose of development is connected with the flourishing of the non-human
world. For a discussion on humans made in the image of God and its implications for international development, see Theos, CAFOD and Tearfund (2010).
See also Deane-Drummond (2019b), who argues that the belief of humans made
in the image of God entails a narrative of uniqueness, or distinctive human dignity, within one of interconnectedness in which other creatures also bear some
forms of dignity.
17 The literature on *buen vivir* (good living) is extensive, including regarding its
risks of being co-opted by political agendas which favour extractivism. See,
among others, Beling et al. (2018), Vanhulst and Beling (2014, 2019), Villalba-
Eguiluz and Iker Etxano (2017).
18 David Attenborough, *A Life on our Planet*, documentary broadcast in 2020 on
Netflix. For a discussion on wisdom in the context of environmental degradation, see Deane-Drummond (2006, 2019a, 2019b).
19 See www.theguardian.com/environment/blog/2013/feb/12/pope-benedict-xvi-first-
green-pontiff; www.nationalgeographic.com/news/2013/2/130228-environmental-
pope-green-efficiency-vatican-city (accessed 9 January 2021).
20 Angaangaq Angakkorsuaq, Song of the Wind, performed at a conference on
'Religions and the Sustainable Development Goals', 6–8 March 2019, Vatican City.
21 See Shadle (2018: chapter 13) for a discussion on John Paul II and structures
of sin.

22 See, for example, the Agua Zarca hydro-electric dam in Honduras which led to the murder of indigenous activist Berta Cáceres and other similar conflicts in the Brazilian Amazon (Riethof 2017). There are currently more than 200 socio-environmental conflicts in relation to hydro-electric power (Del Bene, Scheidel and Temper 2018).

23 For the case of the lithium extraction in Northern Chile and demands for electric cars, see, among others, Liu and Agusdinata (2020).

24 For a discussion of the 'see-judge-act' methodology of the Catholic social tradition in dialogue with Sen's capability approach, see Deneulin and Zampini-Davies (2017).

25 For a discussion on the use of religious narratives in Sen's works and the role of parables in the Catholic social tradition, see Deneulin and Zampini-Davies (2020).

26 For the prophetic attitude of St Francis and his spiritual revolution in Christianity of turning round the dominion of man over nature, see White (1967). This 50-year old five-page article already foresaw the content of *Laudato Si'*.

27 Lane (2019: 41) describes the process of falling in love with nature as moving from being a user to becoming an explorer, to becoming a celebrant, and to becoming a lover and seeking union (see also LS 234).

28 For rest as a biological rhythm and its importance for environmental action, see Deane-Drummond (2004, 2017), Grey (2020).

29 See, among others, the summary 'Gender and Climate Change' published in 2015 by the International Union Conservation of Nature, www.iucn.org/sites/dev/files/import/downloads/gender_and_climate_change_issues_brief_cop21__04122015.pdf, accessed 9 January 2021; the summary by the United Nations Framework Convention on Climate Change at https://unfccc.int/gender, accessed 9 January 2021; the overview report on gender and climate change by Emmeline Skinner by the Institute of Development Studies at www.bridge.ids.ac.uk/bridge-publications/cutting-edge-packs/gender-and-climate-change; the UN Report published in July 2020 on Gender, Climate and Security at https://news.un.org/en/story/2020/06/1065982, accessed 9 January 2021.

30 The World Health Organization estimated that in 2017 approximately 810 women died every day from preventable causes related to pregnancy and childbirth; see www.who.int/news-room/fact-sheets/detail/maternal-mortality, accessed 9 January 2021.

31 www.synod.va/content/sinodoamazonico/en/documents/final-document-of-the-amazon-synod.html, accessed 9 January 2021.

References

Araya, Monica. 2020. "Costa Rica as Pioneer of Green Social Contract," in Claude Henry, Johan Rockström and Nicholas Stern (eds), *Standing Up for a Sustainable World. Voices of Change*, Cheltenham: Edward Elgar, www.elgaronline.com/view/edcoll/9781800371774/9781800371774.xml.

Beattie, Tina. 2016. "Maternal Well-Being in Sub-Saharan Africa: From Silent Suffering to Human Flourishing", in Agbonkhianmeghe Orobator (ed), *The Church We Want: African Catholics Look to Vatican III*, Maryknoll, NY: Orbis Press, pp. 175–88.

Beling, Adrián et al. 2018. "Discursive Synergies for a 'Great Transformation' Towards Sustainability: Pragmatic Contributions to a Necessary Dialogue Between Human Development, Degrowth, and Buen Vivir," *Ecological Economics* 144: 304–13, https://doi.org/10.1016/j.ecolecon.2017.08.025.

Capra, Fritjof and Ove Daniel Jakobsen. 2017. "A Conceptual Framework for Ecological Economics Based on Systemic Principles of Life," *International Journal of Social Economics* 44(6): 831–44, https://doi-org.ezproxy1.bath.ac.uk/10.1108/IJSE-05-2016-0136.

Capra, Fritjof and Pier Luigi Luisi. 2016. *The Systems View of Life: A Unifying Vision*, Cambridge: Cambridge University Press.

Castillo, Daniel P. 2019. *An Ecological Theology of Liberation: Salvation and Political Theology*, Maryknoll: Orbis Books.

Deane-Drummond, Celia. 2004. "Living from the Sabbath: Developing an Ecological Theology in the Context of Biodiversity," in Denis Edwards and Mark Worthing (eds), *Biodiversity and Ecology as Interdisciplinary Challenge*, Adelaide, ATF Press, pp. 1–13.

———— 2006. *Wonder and Wisdom: Conversations in Science, Spirituality and Theology*, London: Darton, Longman and Todd.

———— 2017. *A Primer in Ecotheology: Theology for a Fragile Earth*, Eugene, OR: Cascade Books.

———— 2019a. "A Recovery of Practical Wisdom for Sustainable Futures," in *CUSP Essay Series on the Morality of Sustainable Prosperity*, Centre for the Understanding of Sustainable Prosperity, No. 8, University of Surrey, cusp.ac.uk/essay/m1–8.

———— 2019b. *Theological Ethics through a Multispecies Lens: The Evolution of Wisdom*, Volume 1, Oxford: Oxford University Press.

Del Bene, Daniela, Arnim Scheidel and Leah Temper. 2018. "More Dams, More Violence? A Global Analysis on Resistances and Repression around Conflictive Dams through Co-Produced Knowledge," *Sustainability Science* 13: 617–33, https://doi.org/10.1007/s11625-018-0558-1.

Deneulin, Séverine. 2006. *The Capability Approach and the Praxis of Development*, Basingstoke: Palgrave Macmillan.

————. 2008. "Beyond Individual Agency and Freedom: Structures of Living Together in the Capability Approach," in S. Alkire, M. Qizilbash and F. Comim (eds), *The Capability Approach: Concepts, Measures and Applications*, Cambridge: Cambridge University Press, pp. 105–24.

———— 2014. *Wellbeing, Justice and Development Ethics*, Abingdon: Routledge.

Deneulin, Séverine and Augusto Zampini-Davies. 2017. "Engaging Development with Religion: Methodological Groundings," *World Development* 99: 110–21, doi.org/10.1016/j.worlddev.2017.07.014.

————. 2020. "Religion and the Capability Approach," in Enrica Chiappero-Martinetti, Siddiq Osmani and Mozaffar Qizilbash (eds), *A Handbook of the Capability Approach*, Cambridge: Cambridge University Press, pp. 689–708.

Drèze, Jean and Amartya Sen. 2013. *An Uncertain Glory: India and its Contradictions*, London: Allen Lane.

Gasper, Des and Irene van Staveren. 2003. "Development as Freedom – and as What Else?" *Feminist Economics* 9(2/3): 137–62, doi: 10.1080/1354570032000078663.

Giraud, Gael, Hélène L'Huillier and Cécile Renouard. 2018. "Crisis and Relief in the Niger Delta (2012–13): Assessment of the Effects of a Flood on Relational Capabilities," *Oxford Development Studies* 46(1): 113–31, https://doi.org/10.1080/13600818.2017.1328046.

Grey, Carmody. 2020. "Time and Measures of Success: Interpreting and Implementing Laudato Si'," *New Blackfriars* 101(1091): 5–28, https://doi.org/10.1111/nbfr.12498.

Hansen, Luke. 2019. "Catholic Sisters and Nuns Call for Voting Rights for Women at the Amazon Synod," *America Magazine*, 4 October, www.americamagazine.org/faith/2019/10/04/catholic-sisters-and-nuns-call-voting-rights-women-amazon-synod (Accessed 9 January 2021).

Hoffmann, Nimi and Thaddeus Metz. 2017. "What Can the Capabilities Approach Learn from an Ubuntu Ethic? A Relational Approach to Development Theory," *World Development* 97: 153–64, https://doi.org/10.1016/j.worlddev.2017.04.010.

Hollenbach, David. 2002. *The Common Good and Christian Ethics*, Cambridge: Cambridge University Press.

Ibrahim, Solava. 2020. "Individualism and the Capability Approach: The Role of Collectivities in Expanding Human Capabilities," in Enrica Chiappero-Martinetti, Siddiqui Osmani and Mozaffar Qizilbash (eds), *The Cambridge Handbook of the Capability Approach*, Cambridge: Cambridge University Press, pp. 206–26.

Kopenawa, Davi, Albert Bruce and Alison Dundy. 2013. *The Falling Sky: Words of a Yanomami Shaman*, Cambridge, MA: Harvard University Press.

Kramm, Matthias. 2020. "When a River Becomes a Person," *Journal of Human Development and Capabilities*: 1–13, https://doi.org/10.1080/19452829.2020.1801610.

Lane, Belden C. 2019. *The Great Conversation: Nature and the Care for the Soul*, New York: Oxford University Press.

Larsen, Peter Bille. 2019. "The Dog in the Manger: Neoliberal Slogans at War in the Peruvian Amazon," in Nicolette Makovicky, Anne- Christine Trémon and Sheyla S. Zandonai (ed), *Slogans: Subjection, Subversion, and the Politics of Neoliberalism*, Abingdon: Routledge, pp. 101–21, https://archive-ouverte.unige.ch/unige:111267.

Leifsen, Esben. 2017. "Wasteland by Design: Dispossession by Contamination and the Struggle for Water Justice in the Ecuadorian Amazon," *The Extractive Industries and Society* 4(2): 344–51, https://doi.org/10.1016/j.exis.2017.02.001.

Liu, Wenjuan and Datu Agusdinata. 2020. "Interdependencies of Lithium Mining and Communities Sustainability in Salar de Atacama, Chile," *Journal of Cleaner Production* 260: 1–13, doi: 10.1016/j.jclepro.2020.120838.

Lovejoy, Thomas and Carlos Nobre. 2018. "Amazon Tipping Point," *Science Advances* 4(2): 2340, doi: 10.1126/sciadv.aat2340.

Lytle, Mark. 2007. *The Gentle Subversive: Rachel Carson, Silent Spring, and the Rise of the Environmental Movement*, New York: Oxford University Press.

Niinimäki, K. et al. 2020. "The Environmental Price of Fast Fashion", *Nature Reviews Earth & Environment*, 1: 189–200, www.nature.com/articles/s43017-020-0039-9.

Nobre, I. and Nobre C. 2019. *Amazon 4.0 Project: Defining a Third Way for the Amazon*, Fundação FHC, https://medium.com/funda%C3%A7%C3%A3o-fhc/amazon-4-0-project-defining-a-third-path-for-the-amazon-f0412305f066 (Accessed 9 January 2021).

Nussbaum, Martha. 2011. *Creating Capabilities: The Human Development Project*, Cambridge, MA: Harvard University Press.

Pontifical Council for Justice and Peace (PCJP). 2005. *Compendium of the Social Doctrine of the Church*, www.vatican.va/roman_curia/pontifical_councils/justpeace/documents/rc_pc_justpeace_doc_20060526_compendio-dott-soc_en.html.

Raworth, Kate. 2018. *Doughnut Economics*, London: RH Business Books, www.kateraworth.com/doughnut/.

Ricoeur, Paul. 1992. *One Self as Another*, Chicago: University of Chicago Press.

Riethof, Marieke. 2017. "The International Human Rights Discourse as a Strategic Focus in Socio-Environmental Conflicts: The Case of Hydro-Electric Dams in Brazil," *The International Journal of Human Rights* 21(4): 482–99, https://doi.org/10.1080/13642987.2016.1191775.

Robeyns, Ingrid. 2008. "Sen's Capability Approach and Feminist Concerns," in Sabina Alkire, Mozaffar Qizilbash and Flavio Comim (eds), *The Capability Approach: Concepts, Measures and Applications*, Cambridge: Cambridge University Press, pp, 82–104, https://doi.org/10.1017/CBO9780511492587.004.

———. 2017. *Wellbeing, Freedom and Social Justice: The Capability Approach Re-Examined*, Cambridge: Open Book Publishers, www.openbookpublishers.com/product/682.

Scheid, Daniel. 2016. *The Cosmic Common Good: Religious Grounds for Ecological Ethics*, Oxford: Oxford University Press.

Sen, Amartya. 1999. *Development as Freedom*, Oxford: Oxford University Press.

———. 2002. "Response to Commentaries," *Studies in Comparative International Development* 37(2): 78–86, https://doi.org/10.1007/bf02686264.

———. 2009. *The Idea of Justice*, London: Allen Lane.

———. 2013. "What is it Like to be Like a Human Being?" in *United Nations Development Programme, Human Development Report 2013: The Rise of the South: Human Progress in a Diverse World*, p. 24, http://hdr.undp.org/en/content/what-it-be-human-being.

———. 2015. *The Country of First Boys and Other Essays*, New Delhi: Oxford University Press.

———. 2017. *Collective Choice and Social Welfare*, London: Allen Lane.

Shadle, Matthew. 2018. *Interrupting Capitalism: Catholic Social Teaching and the Economy*, New York: Oxford University Press.

Stewart, Frances. 2005. "Groups and Capabilities," *Journal of Human Development and Capabilities* 6(2): 185–204, https://doi-org.ezproxy1.bath.ac.uk/10.1080/14649880500120517.

———. 2020. "Overcoming Short-Termism: Incorporating Future Generations into Current Decision-Making," *Irish Studies in International Affairs* 31: 1–17, https://doi.org/10.3318/ISIA.2020.31.04.

Stewart, Frances and Séverine Deneulin. 2002. "Amartya Sen's Contribution to Development Thinking," *Studies in Comparative International Development* 37(2): 61–70, https://doi-org.ezproxy1.bath.ac.uk/10.1007/BF02686262.

Theos, CAFOD and Tearfund. 2020. *Wholly Living: A New Perspective on International Development*, www.theosthinktank.co.uk/research/2010/10/10/wholly-living-a-new-perspective-on-international-development.

United Nations Development Programme (UNDP). 2016. *Human Development Report: Human Development for Everyone*, www.hdr.undp.org/en/content/human-development-report-2016.

———. 2019. *Human Development Report: Beyond Income, Beyond Averages, Beyond Today: Inequalities in Human Development in the 21st Century*, www.hdr.undp.org/en/2019-report.

———. 2020. *Human Development Report. The Next Frontier: Human Development and the Anthropocene*, http://hdr.undp.org/.

Vanhulst, Julien and Adrian Beling. 2014. "Buen Vivir: Emergent Discourse within or Beyond Sustainable Development?" *Ecological Economics*, 101: 54–63, https://doi.org/10.1016/j.ecolecon.2014.02.017.

———. 2019. "Post-Eurocentric Sustainability Governance: Lessons from the Latin American Buen Vivir Experiment," in Agni Kalfagianni, Doris Fuchs, Anders Hayden (eds), *Routledge Handbook of Global Sustainability Governance*, Abingdon: Routledge, pp. 115–28.

Villalba-Eguiluz, Unai and Iker Etxano. 2017. "Buen Vivir vs Development (II): The Limits of (Neo-)Extractivism," *Ecological Economics*, 138: 1–11, https://doi.org/10.1016/j.ecolecon.2017.03.010.

Walker, Melanie. 2020. "The Well-Being of South African University Students from Low-Income Households," *Oxford Development Studies* 48(1): 56–69, https://doi.org/10.1080/13600818.2019.1672143.

Watene, Krushil. 2016. "Valuing Nature: Māori Philosophy and the Capability Approach," *Oxford Development Studies* 44(3): 287–97, https://doi.org/10.1080/13600818.2015.1124077.

White, Lynn Jr. 1967. "The Historical Roots of Our Ecologic Crisis," *Science*, 155(3767): 1203–7, www.jstor.org/stable/1720120.

World Health Organization (WHO). 2017. *Inheriting a Sustainable World: Atlas on Children's Health and the Environment*, www.who.int/ceh/publications/inheriting-a-sustainable-world/en/.

3 Transformational pathways

At the core of the concept of development lies the idea of change or transformation and making situations better. Analysing and transforming situations, in order to make them less unjust, have been defining concerns of development research.[1] But in order to transform, one needs a horizon, or some normative goals, to guide action. The SDGs could be candidates, but they are not without criticisms (cf. Introduction). Some goals seem incompatible, while the achievement of others requires systemic transformations that are not highlighted. For example, achieving SDG 3 (good health) entails a reform of health systems to guarantee universal access; or achieving SDG 5 (gender equality) requires cultural change of patriarchal and sexist attitudes and behaviours; or achieving SDG13 (taking action to combat climate change and its impacts) requires structural transformation at all levels of society, including combatting what Pope Francis has called a 'throwaway culture' (LS 16, 22, 43, FT 188).

Sen's approach to development does not specify goals as to what situations are to be transformed into or a blueprint to identify what counts as an injustice to be remedied (cf. Chapter 1). Does, for example, a situation of loneliness and isolation among elderly people count as an injustice in the same way as a situation where children are poisoned by pesticides or toxic residues from mining? Or does a situation of employment through zero-hour contracts count as an injustice in the same way as a situation where people work as day labourers in dangerous work conditions? Sen's capability approach may offer a basis for thinking about questions of justice, but it does not, as such, answer these questions. All it does is propose an interpretative evaluation framework to compare situations, without being prescriptive about what a just situation would look like, or which goals to aim at, beyond implicitly affirming that a desirable goal is to ensure that every person is able to live a 'minimally acceptable life', or live a life she has reason to value. It is even less prescriptive about which transformational pathways to take towards that goal. Rather than condemning a situation where people die of easily preventable diseases, or a situation where

DOI: 10.4324/9781003121534-4

people work in slave labour conditions, as morally wrong, Sen's approach simply argues for assessing situations in the capability space, that is, in terms of what people are able to do and to be, such as the extent to which they are able to avoid a premature death, have decent work, or have meaningful social relationships. It then advocates submitting that information to processes of public reasoning. The idea of 'public reasoning' and 'agency' is central to Sen's approach. How to promote development, how to combat situations of poverty and inequality, in all their forms, and how to combat situations of environmental degradation ultimately rest on public reasoning and on people's agency, which he defines as 'the ability of people to help themselves and to influence the world' (Sen 1999: 18).

This chapter examines some of the favoured remedial actions that Sen has been discussing in his works under the broad term of public action. It highlights the importance of the marginalized organizing themselves politically, public discussion on what affects the lives of the disadvantaged, and the nurturing of a sense of solidarity. It also critically discusses the role of power and some of the concerns that have been raised about Sen's works lacking realism or being too optimistic about the reach of human reason. The chapter then discusses how the Catholic social tradition perceives public action. It underlines similarities, such as a focus on institutional analysis and the central role of human agency to transform institutions. It also draws some differences of emphasis, such as the orientation of public action towards the common good, what the Catholic tradition calls social or political love, a focus on accompaniment of marginalized communities, and the anchoring of public reasoning in a culture of encounter, attentiveness, and self-examination. It concludes by examining how Sen's account of reducing injustice could inform the Catholic Church's own transformational journey towards integral human development.

Transformational pathways in Sen's conception of development

Public action: listening, organizing, and solidarity

Amartya Sen never intended to propose a theory of development or a theory of justice that would offer a comprehensive framework for how development is to be promoted or injustice reduced. One could say that what Sen offers is a public reasoning approach to justice based on his capability approach: that is, that

> it is through public reason that we come to know about justice at all. Whether we want to know . . . about ideally just social relations, or

about thresholds for adequate justice, we have only public reason with which to seek that knowledge.

(Drydyk 2020a: 676)

His *Idea of Justice* (Sen 2009) countered the argument that one needed to answer the questions of 'What is a just society? And what 'just institutions look like, in order to start remedying injustice.[2] Sen's preferred transformational pathway is not achieved by assessing how current institutions fall short of an ideal. For example, he does not assess the extent to which a public health system falls short of giving every person equal access to treatment irrespective of socio-economic status or race. Rather, he offers an evaluative framework to assess how well institutions are doing and how more just or less unjust they are insofar as they facilitate or undermine the conditions for people to live well. We find an example of this in relation to health. Sen (2015) does not discuss transformational pathways to advance greater equity in health globally. What he does instead is compare health attainments across some countries (Rwanda, Thailand, Bangladesh) and some states of India (Kerala, Himachal Pradesh, and Tamil Nadu), and then examine which health policy decisions have been taken in those countries and states, considering their own political and economic contexts. Through this comparison, he concludes that improved health outcomes can be achieved, despite low economic resources, when there is a public commitment to invest in universal primary healthcare and when those without access to private health insurance are politically well represented.

In their works on analysing the situation of India with the capability approach, Jean Drèze and Amartya Sen have discussed many examples which illustrate the crucial role of what they call 'public action' for changing the way institutions function and for orienting them towards providing the conditions for human flourishing (Drèze and Sen 1989, 1995, 2002, 2013, 2020). They broadly define public action as the direct efforts undertaken by the public at large to improve their lives, and these can take many forms. Sen (2019: 356) talks of 'public action' as 'involving not just the government but also the public itself – in all its manifold economic, social, and political activities'. One transformational pathway Drèze and Sen highlight throughout their joint works is the political representation of the marginalized and the presence of organizations with which they can advance their claims. In the case of Kerala (Drèze and Sen 2013), the people of disadvantaged castes have been able to get politically organized, and therefore they have been able to orient public spending towards investment in primary healthcare and demand greater accountability and citizen scrutiny of public spending, leading to less corruption. The successes of the Indian state of Kerala in dealing with Covid-19 and in managing low morbidity rates, epidemiological control, and low economic and social costs continue to reflect this public commitment combined with high levels of community participation in policy decision-making (Menon et al. 2020).

Another transformational pathway Sen has singled out throughout his works is the importance of public discussion and a free press. Sen's works on the relationship between famines and public discussion are well known. Famines, he argued, are caused not by food shortages as such but by a failure of democracy.[3] The following passage from *Development as Freedom* best summarizes Sen's views on public action and its importance as a transformational pathway:

> The response of a government to the acute suffering of its people often depends on the pressure that is put on it. The exercise of political rights (such as voting, criticizing, protesting, and the like) can make a real difference to the political incentives that operate on a government. I have discussed elsewhere the remarkable fact that, in the terrible history of famines in the world, no substantial famine has ever occurred in any independent and democratic country with a relatively free press. We cannot find exceptions to this rule, no matter where we look.
>
> (Sen 1999: 7)

In a review of Drèze and Sen's works and what kinds of transformational pathways they have identified for making situations less unjust, Alkire (2006) highlights the following: public action and participation, value formation and value change, and the cultivation of bonds of solidarity between those who are more privileged and those who are less. She also highlights the importance of public outcry in the face of human suffering, that is, the capacity of the public to feel outraged at a situation such as the prevalence of malnutrition among India's children and be moved to do something about it.

As Chapter 2 discussed, empathy is a critical feature of the anthropological vision underpinning Sen's conception of development, but it puts equal emphasis on the importance of the marginalized voicing what ails their lives and of others being able to listen to that pain or cry. In Sen's works, people who suffer from capability deprivation, such as the ability to be adequately nourished, are not only patients in need of attention but also agents who can transform society themselves. It is therefore not surprising that he puts equal weight on the expression of suffering as its listening. As the concluding sentences of Drèze and Sen's book *Hunger and Public Action* express it:

> It is essential to see the public not merely as 'the patient' whose well-being commands attention, but also as 'the agent' whose actions can

transform society. Taking note of that dual role is central to understanding the challenge of public action against hunger.

(Drèze and Sen 1989: 279)

In another writing, Sen (2019: 356) reiterates the argument that the 'public is, above all, the agent of change, and not a patient to be looked after and ordered about'.

Throughout her review, Alkire (2006) emphasizes the non-prescriptive nature of Sen and Drèze's transformational pathways, the innumerable ways in which agency could be exercised, and the many forms actions could take given the local context and unjust situation to address. In the case of hunger in India, Drèze and Sen (2002: 336–40) point to the need to change the government's policy of a minimum price for food producers, as it has led to large amounts of grain being stocked, even left to rot, as the government itself had to buy surplus food to maintain prices. They advocate that the government should launch a programme of food distribution from these government-maintained stocks in order to address hunger; and Sen continues to call for such food distribution policy, such as 'drawing on the 60 million tons of rice and wheat that remain unused in the godowns of the Food Corporation of India', to address the loss of livelihoods caused by the Covid-19 pandemic (Sen 2020a). Drèze and Sen also advocate that subsistence farmers organize politically to counteract the policy influence of better-organized large-scale farmers who have been able to lobby the government for this guaranteed food price policy. A 'fair distribution of power', they conclude, 'is a basic – indeed fundamental – requirement of democracy' (Drèze and Sen 2002: 353). This is why they emphasize the types of action that can decrease the power of some (e.g. large-scale farmers and agribusinesses) and increase the power of others (e.g. subsistence farmers and day labourers). They note that a particularly powerful tool to that effect has been, in the case of India, the Right to Information Act,[4] which has led to corruption and power abuses being brought to light. They cite the example of the corporate influence of the Biscuit Manufacturers' Association on the school meal policy. The Act allowed for the wider public to be informed about members of the Indian Parliament being sent letters which described the benefits of manufactured food and urged them to replace with manufactured biscuits the government-financed programme of school meals cooked by local people using locally produced food.

Another pathway Drèze and Sen (2002: 28) highlight, in order to address power inequality and to bring the concerns of the marginalized to the heart of policymaking, is to build a sense of

solidarity with the underprivileged on the part of other members of society, whose interests and commitments are broadly linked, and who are often better placed to advance the cause of the disadvantaged by virtue of their own privileges (e.g. those with access to formal education, the media, economic resources, and political connections).

However, they warn that a focus on speaking on behalf of the voiceless by well-intentioned people or organizations risks diverting attention from poor people's own voiced concerns and that the solidarity route may not always 'be entirely congruent with the interests of those whom they seek to represent' (Drèze and Sen 2002: 30) – hence the need to enable those who are marginalized to voice their concerns themselves and to organize politically to make their voices heard.

Two recent opinion pieces by Amartya Sen on policy responses to the global pandemic illustrate the transformational dynamic here. In an article published online in *The Indian Express* magazine and originally entitled 'Listening as Governance',[5] Sen (2020a) reiterates his arguments about the role of democratic elections and public discussion in overcoming famines. Again, he emphasizes the crucial role of speaking and listening:

> Even though only a minority may actually face the deprivation of a famine, a listening majority, informed by public discussion and a free press, can make a government responsive. This can happen either through sympathy (when the government cares), or through the antipathy that would be generated by its inaction (when the government remains uncaring).

Taking this argument to the current global pandemic and the loss of employment and income that the poor and the most vulnerable are experiencing more acutely, Sen concludes that 'listening is central in the government's task of preventing social calamity – hearing what the problems are, where exactly they have hit, and how they affect the victims'. In another short opinion piece published in the *Financial Times*, Sen (2020b) draws once more from history, this time from post-war Britain, to illustrate the critical role of public action in transforming a crisis into an opportunity for improved nutrition and healthcare access. He notes that food shortages during the Second World War led to more equitable food sharing through rationing policies, with the result of life expectancy in England and Wales rising by 6.5 years for men and 7 years for women during the 1940s (compared with a 1.2 year and 1.5 year rise, respectively, during the 1930s). The crisis of the Second World War, Sen (2020b) underlines, also led Aneurin Bevan to plan for a National Health Service to make access to healthcare free for all.

Characteristically, Sen is not prescriptive about which actions to take and how best to express concern for the lives of the marginalized, beyond ensuring that their concerns are not forgotten in public discussions and their voices are heard by those who have the power to make decisions. A basic premise of Sen's arguments is the existence of democratic practice, which requires that the voices of the marginalized and of those who seek to address their concerns are not silenced, whether by violence or intimidation, or dismissed. The question therefore arises of how Sen's arguments about the critical roles of speaking, listening, public discussion, and empathy could play out in a context where those who organize to voice their concerns receive death threats or are killed, such as where people are displaced from their land by extractive industries, agribusinesses, or infrastructure projects.[6]

Public reasoning and power

In his review of Sen's life and works, Hamilton (2019) remains sceptical of the reach of Sen's ideas about reasoning and public discussion as a transformational pathway for reducing injustice amidst unequal political and economic power relations. He argues that Sen 'lays to one side – as economist and philosopher – the trenchant questions of power, and how it is propagated and who wields it. . . . He assumes that the best argument will always win' (Hamilton 2019: 20). He concludes that

> Sen's faith in public reason leaves him blind to the fact that the problem may not be just 'valuational plurality' and associated stubborn conflict, even despite the 'confrontation with reason', but that conflict may have its source in irrevocably partisan interests that undermine the very idea of impartiality that lies at the heart of Sen's account of justice.
> (Hamilton 2019: 119–20)

Sen's faith in the reach of public reasoning, or public discussion, for remedying injustice is indeed strong. As Chapter 1 described, when confronted with the decision of which valuable goal to pursue given the plurality of values (valuational plurality) – for example, whether to introduce legislation to protect an endangered animal species such as the spotted owl – he settles the matter through, what he calls, public reasoning. Despite seeing public reasoning as 'central . . . to the pursuit of social justice' (Sen 2009: 44), he has remained reluctant to define it. When asked for a definition, he replied that one did not need a definition of public reasoning to conclude that the American elections in November 2016, which brought Trump as president, and the UK Brexit referendum in June 2016 were not examples of 'good' public reasoning processes.[7]

Sen maintains a strong conviction that better arguments will always win through more and better public reasoning, as he puts it in *The Idea of Justice*:

> The pervasiveness of unreason presents good grounds for scepticism about the practical effectiveness of reasoned discussion of confused social subjects. . . . This particular scepticism of the reach of reasoning does not yield any ground for not using reason to the extent one can, in pursuing the idea of justice. . . . Unreason is mostly not the practice of doing without reasoning altogether, but of relying on a very primitive and very defective reasoning. There is hope in this since bad reasoning can be confronted by better reasoning.
>
> (Sen 2009: xvii–xviii)

When faced with the reality of the Amazon region reaching a tipping point and losing its capacity to be a carbon sink (Lovejoy and Nobre 2018), and Brazilian electors voting for a government that promotes deforestation through supporting infrastructure projects, encouraging mining exploration, or incentivizing agribusinesses (Bebbington et al. 2019), there may not be much ground for hope in 'better reasoning' confronting 'bad reasoning'. Another example which would defy Sen's conviction of the reach of public reasoning in addressing injustice is that of public protests and road closures led by representative organizations of agribusinesses to demand the reversal of a policy that limits pesticide use to protect children's health in Paraguay (Correia 2019: 327). Drèze and Sen have never talked of 'good' versus 'bad' public action. Obviously, some collective action may go against the interests of some but not of others, but it is unlikely that public protests to block a policy that would protect children's health would qualify as 'public action' in their use of the word.

In furthering Sen's conception of public reasoning, Drydyk (2020a, 2020b) argues that a judgement on how power is exercised is central to Sen's understanding of 'public', and that a judgement on how power is held to account and whether policies can be justified (i.e. whether they can be supported by evidence and are concerned with people's lives, especially those most vulnerable and marginalized) is central to Sen's understanding of 'reasoning' (Drydyk 2020b). Drydyk's characterization of public reasoning in Sen's works is helpful, but it does not address the critique of power and how power relations can affect the public reasoning process. As Hamilton highlights, Sen's *Idea of Justice* does not provide tools to analyse power relations and to assess their disruptive effects on decision-making processes (Hamilton 2019: 91). It also 'underplays the importance of institutions in the formation and regulation of behaviour, that is, in the formation of preferences, choices, and values' (Hamilton 2019: 135) – for example, how social media influences the formation of values.[8] Another critique he raises of Sen's works is that they have dealt much more with how goods are converted by humans into valuable capabilities – for example, how food is converted into the functioning of being healthy – than with the processes through which these goods are produced – for example, whether food has been produced by immigrants working in slave labour conditions (Hamilton 2019: 159). Sen's works have also dealt little with markets as institutional mechanisms for the exchange of goods, particularly financial markets. He has continued to argue that markets and how they function have to be assessed according to their consequences for people's lives. The degree of market regulation depends on how it will improve the lives of the poorest (Sen 1993, 1999). While writing extensively on hunger and malnutrition, Sen has never advanced a position regarding which types of institutional mechanisms, and agricultural and food systems, are better for addressing hunger, beyond affirming the need for both state intervention and well-functioning markets.[9]

On the one hand, Hamilton's critiques are justified, for Sen's works have indeed not dealt much with the configuration of power relations and with how global production systems undermine human dignity and damage ecosystems.[10] Neither have they dealt with the role institutions play in constructing people's values. On the other hand, Sen's works never intended to provide a complete theory of justice, or a theory of development, and the task of going deeper into analysis of power and how institutions shape people's values, for better or for worse, is deliberately left unfinished. This task is for others. There is a growing literature on education which examines how educational institutions affect value formation from the perspective of the capability approach. Vaughan and Walker (2012) have argued for a form of education that makes students aware of their values and that submits them to critical thinking and encounter with others. Walker and Wilson-Strydom (2016) explore the types of pedagogies in higher education that form students as agents of social transformation and how universities could contribute to making societies more socially just.[11] McGrath (2018) examines the role education plays in development more broadly, and he discusses how certain visions of development and understandings of what education is for are linked. Tilky (2020) discusses the role of education in fostering more socially just and sustainable societies. Sen himself is an illustration of how certain types of education foster certain values and how education can be a key transformational pathway for value change and for motivating action for social justice. He has often credited his formative years in Santiniketan, and the influence of Rabindranath Tagore, as instilling in him the importance of freedom, of a humanity that included everyone, and the danger of ascribing to people a single identity (Khan 2012; Sen 2006, 2020c).

If there is one critique that remains justified, it is that Sen's faith in the reach of human reason is strong. Whether human reason is sufficient to overcome the socio-environmental challenges we are witnessing is an open question. In reviewing Tagore's foundational influence on Sen's thinking, Khan (2012) noted that Tagore conceived the human person as having

> two polarities that must be kept in harmony. At one pole, the strength is 'in the fullness of its community with all things'. . . . At the other, the strength is in self-transcendence in which the self reveals to itself its own meaning.
>
> (Khan 2012: 6)

Khan concluded that Sen had given much more weight to the pole of the self which reveals meaning through its own power than to the pole of the self that is oriented towards communion with others. For Tagore, 'man is a spiritual being' (quoted in Khan 2012: 5) whose meaning also comes from beyond himself through, among other ways, art and poetry.[12] In *Laudato Si'*, Pope Francis argued that, in order to address complex socio-environmental challenges, 'no branch of the sciences and no form of wisdom can be left out' (LS 63). This includes not only art and poetry but also languages particular to religion. The next section explores what one such form of wisdom could offer to Sen's understanding of public reason and public action as transformational pathways.

Transformational pathways in the Catholic social tradition

Public action: charity, social love, and accompaniment

Like Amartya Sen, the Catholic social tradition proposes an approach and not a theory of development or justice. Like Sen's perspective, it favours a method of social action that starts with assessing situations and the kinds of lives that people live, which it calls the 'seeing' stage. Like Sen's, it then proceeds to evaluating the institutional arrangements behind these situations, which it calls the 'judging' stage. However, as Chapter 2 discussed, for the Catholic social tradition, it is not only situations which are less, or more, just, in terms of their outcomes but also institutions or structures. In words reminiscent of Sen's, that 'our opportunities and prospects depend crucially on what institutions exist and how they function' (Sen 1999: 142), *Laudato Si'* affirms that 'the health of a society's institutions has consequences for the environment and the quality of human life' (LS 142). This is why it argues that 'social ecology is necessarily institutional' (LS 142).

Like in Sen's approach, the Catholic social tradition emphasizes the role of human agency in transforming these institutions that regulate human relationships. Already *Populorum Progressio* talked of 'all peoples [becoming] the artisans of their destiny' (PP 65). *Laudato Si'* talks of 'the ability to work together in building our common home' (LS 13). Like Sen's perspective, the Catholic social tradition is not prescriptive about what sort of actions best transform institutions and make them more conducive to the flourishing of people and ecosystems. It affirms in that regard that 'there are no uniform recipes' (LS 180), there is no one solution to the challenges of poverty (FT 65), and that it is not the task of the Church to offer technical solutions (CV 9). *Laudato Si'* mentions the necessity for many ways forward and some examples of kinds of action that can be taken, including 'enforceable international agreements' and 'global regulatory norms' (LS 173), new forms of economic production (LS 112, 129), and 'developing an economy of waste disposal and recycling' (LS 180), new forms of agriculture which 'defend the interests of small producers and preserve local ecosystems from destruction' (LS 180), producing renewable energy at all levels of society (LS 179), avoiding the use of plastic, not running taps unnecessarily, not throwing food away, using public transport, turning off unnecessary lights (LS 211), and restoring a disused garden or public square (LS 232). 'Truly, much can be done!', it concludes (LS180), and it is up to public discussion to discern which remedial actions to take in one's context.

In the context of the Amazon region, the public reasoning process at the October 2019 Synod concluded the following public action:

> We may not be able to modify the destructive model of extractivist development immediately, but we do need to know and make clear where we stand, whose side we are on, what perspective we assume. For this reason: a) we denounce the violation of human rights and extractive destruction; b) we embrace and support campaigns of divestment from extractive companies responsible for the socio-ecological damage of the Amazon . . . c) we call for a radical energy transition and the search for alternatives.[13]

There is however one difference, or rather a difference of emphasis, between Sen's and the Catholic social tradition's account of public action. As mentioned earlier, there is an implicit assumption in Sen's works that public action, as action by the public at large, is not any action but that which has at its centre the concern of those who live in conditions of marginalization and exclusion. The Catholic social tradition is more forthright about the ends that public action serves, namely the common good, and connects acting with loving:

> To love someone is to desire that person's good and to take effective steps to secure it. Besides the good of the individual, there is a good that is linked to living in society: the common good. It is the good of all of us.
>
> (CV 7)

Actions for the good of a concrete individual person (love) cannot be separated from actions for the good of all (social, civil, or political love); they are in dynamic interaction:

> Love, overflowing with small gestures of mutual care, is also civic and political, and it makes itself felt in every action that seeks to build a better world. Love for society and commitment to the common good are outstanding expressions of a charity which affects not only relationships between individuals but also macro-relationships, social, economic and political ones.
>
> (LS 231)

Actions that promote human rights for all are expressions of such political love (FT 22), as are actions aimed at reducing inequality. The two paragraphs quoted here from *Fratelli Tutti* exemplify this dynamic of seeing, judging, and acting (out of love). First, it assesses situations in the kinds of lives that people live – in this case, many people have their human rights denied, or to put it in a capability language, are unable to live a healthy life, to be adequately sheltered and clothed, to be adequately nourished. It then judges the institutions which lie behind such states of affairs – in this case, an economic ideological structure which prioritizes profits at the expense of people:

> [B]y closely observing our contemporary societies, we see numerous contradictions that lead us to wonder whether the equal dignity of all human beings, solemnly proclaimed seventy years ago, is truly recognized, respected, protected and promoted in every situation. In today's world, many forms of injustice persist, fed by reductive anthropological visions and by a profit-based economic model that does not hesitate to exploit, discard and even kill human beings. While one part of humanity lives in opulence, another part sees its own dignity denied, scorned or trampled upon, and its fundamental rights discarded or

violated. What does this tell us about the equality of rights grounded in innate human dignity?

(FT 22)

It then proceeds to giving a few examples of expression of such political love, which springs from the virtue of charity at the individual level, to transform the situation:

> It is an act of charity to assist someone suffering, but it is also an act of charity, even if we do not know that person, to work to change the social conditions that caused his or her suffering. If someone helps an elderly person cross a river, that is a fine act of charity. The politician, on the other hand, builds a bridge, and that too is an act of charity. While one person can help another by providing something to eat, the politician creates a job for that other person, and thus practices a lofty form of charity that ennobles his or her political activity.

(FT 186)

The Catholic social tradition puts here an equal focus on concrete acts of charity – giving shelter to a homeless person, giving food to someone who is hungry, giving clothing to someone in need, giving medication to someone who is ill, transforming a degraded soil into a fertile one, and so forth – and acts that change the structures which have made someone homeless, hungry, ill, or structures which have degraded soils. Both what Benedict XVI calls in *Caritas in Veritate* 'the institutional path' or 'political path of charity' and the 'kind of charity which encounters the neighbour directly, outside the institutional mediation of the pólis', are 'no less excellent and effective' (CV 7).[14]

Following Paul Ricoeur (1995, 2000), one could describe love, or charity, as characterizing our relationships with those whom we know personally (say, Fernando, an individual farmer one has encountered in El Salvador who has lost all his maize crops to climate change–induced drought), and justice, or social, or political love, as characterizing our relationships with others who have an anonymous face (all the subsistence farmers globally who have lost their livelihoods due to climate change and whose faces one cannot put a name on).[15] Concrete acts of love, or charity, towards Fernando could involve assisting him to mitigate the negative consequences of climate change on his livelihood, such as through training in new agricultural practices that enable him to face extreme weather events or in new forms of work. Concrete acts of justice, or acts of political love, could involve work towards designing international agreements and changing national legislations to curb carbon emissions and limit global temperature rise. Love and justice both need each other. Love is the motivation for action for justice, and action for justice enables love to move from the particular, from the concrete face of a person who has a name, to the universal, to the anonymous faces of many. For the Catholic social tradition, action for justice is always based on love and not on ideology, for, as Pope Francis reminds us in *Fratelli Tutti*, 'we do not serve ideas, we serve people' (FT 115). The parable of the Samaritan, which features as a paradigmatic story for both Sen's capability approach (Sen 2009: 171–2) and the Catholic social tradition (FT 56–86), also exemplifies this creative dialectic between love and justice. For Sen, the action of the Samaritan represented not only an act of love towards a concrete person but also an act of justice and expression of global responsibilities. To the question 'Who is my neighbour?', the answer is 'that we ourselves become neighbours to all' (FT 80).

The relationship between love and justice has not always been in creative tension in the modern history of the Catholic Church. At a time when the world was divided between the communist and capitalist economic systems, it was not uncommon for social and political engagement seeking to transform the structural conditions behind hunger, ill health, or lack of housing, for instance, to be perceived as in collusion with communist sympathies. As the Brazilian archbishop Hélder Câmara was known to have said, when working at changing the structural conditions of poverty in Brazil: 'When I give food to the poor, they call me a saint. When I ask why the poor have no food, they call me a communist.'[16] It is beyond the scope of this book to engage in a critical assessment of the way Latin American theologians dealt with the love–justice dialectic in the 1970s and the 1980s and how they reflected on what love of God and love our neighbour implied in a context marked by authoritarian regimes, large-scale poverty, concentration of wealth and land in the hands of a few, and violent and deadly repression of social protests. Their response in advocating liberation from all forms of oppression and active involvement in political and social struggles for liberation did not always meet sympathetic ears on the part of Church authorities. Cardinal Ratzinger issued two 'Instructions' on liberation theology in the 1980s, condemning its use of Marxism for social and economic analysis, and warning of risks of reducing the universal message of Christ's love to the mere social and political dimension.[17]

As Pope Benedict XVI, in 2009, discussed at length the relation between love (charity) and justice in *Caritas in Veritate*:

> Charity goes beyond justice, because to love is to give, to offer what is 'mine' to the other; but it never lacks justice, which prompts us to give the other what is 'his', what is due to him by reason of his being

or his acting. I cannot 'give' what is mine to the other, without first giving him what pertains to him in justice. If we love others with charity, then first of all we are just towards them. . . . justice is inseparable from charity, and intrinsic to it. . . . On the one hand, charity demands justice: recognition and respect for the legitimate rights of individuals and peoples. . . . On the other hand, charity transcends justice and completes it in the logic of giving and forgiving.

(CV 6)

Thus, the action in the parable of the Samaritan of attending to a wounded stranger on the road is an act of charity that also demands action for justice, for example, by asking why there are people on the road lying injured, which might be because of gangs or other street violence, and then doing something to address violence, or by ensuring that there is always a well-functioning 'inn' (such as a hospital) with appropriate equipment, access to water and electricity, and medication. Charity and justice are inseparable from each other, and a universal healthcare system without charity would be as deficient as charity towards the sick without working at ensuring public health access for all.[18] As Pope Francis comments in *Fratelli Tutti*:

> Even the Good Samaritan . . . needed to have a nearby inn that could provide the help that he was personally unable to offer. Love of neighbour is concrete and squanders none of the resources needed to bring about historical change that can benefit the poor and disadvantaged.

(FT 165)

In talking about such historical and structural change that benefits the poor and disadvantaged, Amartya Sen and Jean Drèze emphasize the capacity of the poor and disadvantaged themselves to mobilize and get politically organized to have their voices heard (cf. supra). As far back as 1891, the encyclical *Rerum Novarum* similarly urged workers to 'form associations among themselves and unite their forces so as to courageously shake off the yoke of such an unrighteous and intolerable oppression' (RN 54). Today, Pope Francis has renewed this emphasis on the poor and disadvantaged organizing themselves in social movements to press for structural change. As he argues in *Fratelli Tutti*:

> Solidarity means much more than engaging in sporadic acts of generosity. . . . It also means combatting the structural causes of poverty, inequality, the lack of work, land and housing, the denial of social and labour rights. It means confronting the destructive effects of the empire

of money. . . . Solidarity, understood in its most profound meaning, is a way of making history.

(FT 116)

When he was Archbishop of Buenos Aires, the then Jorge Bergoglio had been involved in the lives of the waste pickers and other informal sector workers (Azcuy and Cervantes 2014). Since becoming Pope Francis in March 2013, he has continued to support the organizing of informal sector workers and other marginalized workers, such as subsistence farmers, to change the structures which prevent them from obtaining what Sen calls 'a minimally acceptable life'. In October 2014, he convened in the Vatican a World Meeting of Popular Movements as a global platform for social movements from all continents to come together, exchange their experiences, be stronger in their struggles for justice, and become agents of social change.[19] The meeting took place around three themes: land, housing, and work (which in Spanish are known as the 3 Ts, *Techo, Tierra y Trabajo*, sometimes translated in English as the 3 Ls: Land, Lodging, and Livelihood). They have continued to meet annually since then, with the latest meeting taking place online in October 2020, coordinated by the Dicastery for Promoting Integral Human Development.[20] In the Pope's address at their second meeting in Santa Cruz, Bolivia, July 2015, he concluded by affirming:

The future of humanity does not lie solely in the hands of great leaders, the great powers and the elites. It is fundamentally in the hands of peoples and in their ability to organize. It is in their hands, which can guide with humility and conviction this process of change. I am with you.[21]

'Accompaniment' is the term that has been used within the work of Catholic organizations, and other faith-based organizations, to describe this 'I am with you', as an expression of solidarity with the lives of the marginalized.[22] There is however no conceptual treatment yet of 'accompaniment' in the Catholic social tradition. Pope (2019) attributes the shift in the Catholic social tradition – from doing something for the marginalized to being with them – to the life and personal experience of Saint Oscar Romero during the civil war in El Salvador. According to Romero, this presence in the lives of the marginalized was not about 'a politicized apostolate, but rather an apostolate that has to guide the consciences of Christians within a politicized environment' (Romero quoted in Pope 2019: 135).[23] On the basis of Pope Francis's writings and discourses, he defines accompaniment as 'forming relationships of mutual trust based on equal dignity' and then 'mov[ing] to a shared commitment to promote agency' (Pope 2019: 138). The personal experience of Bergoglio, like that of Romero, exemplifies that dynamic of forming relationships of trust with the marginalized residents of Buenos Aires, by simply 'being present to' them by visiting them in their homes, and sharing their commitment to be artisans of their destiny through the organizations that they form. Countless men and women who are not poor have embraced this 'being present to', by forming relationships of mutual trust, and by accompanying those who live in conditions of poverty as agents of structural change, sometimes at the cost of their lives.[24]

The final document of the 2007 meeting of the Latin American bishops' conference in Aparecida, which Bergoglio helped draft, is probably the Church document which comes closest to an account of this 'accompaniment':

> From our faith in Christ, solidarity springs as a permanent attitude of encounter, of brotherhood and service, which finds expressions in visible choices and actions, mainly in the defence of life and the rights of the most vulnerable and excluded, and in the permanent accompaniment of their efforts to be subjects of change and transformation of their situation.
>
> (CELAM 2007, paragraph 394, translation mine)

The document does not however spell out how practically to accompany the vulnerable and excluded in transforming their situation without falling into partisan politics. In his review of various forms of accompaniment, Pope (2019) mentions the work of the Jesuit Refugee Service in Cambodia, which worked both in policy advocacy to introduce an international legislation banning land mines and in supporting the lives of those who have been disabled by land mines. Other examples include the work of religious orders in policy advocacy to end human slavery, in offering assistance to trafficked women globally (Graw Leary 2018), and in changing the cultural norms around female genital mutilation and HIV/AIDS (Clark 2020). Others are the work of churches in community organizing in inner cities in the United States and the United Kingdom (Ivereigh 2010; Ritchie 2019), and the historical work of the Pastoral Land Commission in Brazil, which led to one of the biggest social movements in Latin America, the MST or Landless Rural Workers Movement (Pinto 2015). One could also see the Synod of the Amazon as an initiative of the Church to accompany the people of the Amazon in their defence of life and in defending their rights in the face of land dispossession, human rights abuses, and ecosystem destruction.

Public reasoning: encounter, self-examination, and transformation

This closeness to the lives of the poor and the ability to empathize with what ails their lives as conditions for public reasoning about which remedial action to take were also critical components of Sen's account of public reasoning. Drèze and Sen (2013: 269) called this lack of interest of the privileged in what happens to the lives of the less privileged a 'failure of public reasoning'. The Catholic social tradition does, however, go further by urging that these encounters between the privileged and the less privileged become part of a culture – a way of life:

> To speak of a "culture of encounter" means that we, as a people, should be passionate about meeting others, seeking points of contact, building bridges, planning a project that includes everyone. This becomes an aspiration and a style of life.
>
> (FT 216)

In *Laudato Si'*, Pope Francis deplored the fact that many policy decisions are taken by people who have no close contact with those who are affected by their decisions:

> Many professionals, opinion makers, communications media and centers of power, being located in affluent urban areas, are far removed from the poor, with little direct contact with their problems. They live and reason from the comfortable position of a high level of development and a quality of life well beyond the reach of the majority of the world's population. This lack of physical contact and encounter, . . . can lead to a numbing of conscience and to tendentious analyses which neglect parts of reality.
>
> (LS 49)

'Listening as governance', as Amartya Sen (2020a) puts it, needs to form a culture of listening and of attentiveness to what happens to the lives of others and to the lives of ecosystems. For the Catholic social tradition, cultivating these values of encounter and listening with no agenda, simply being present to the other person, becomes an integral part of development work (Grey 2020). In his post-synodal apostolic exhortation *Querida Amazonia*, Pope Francis talks about listening as a duty of justice (QA 26). Quoting a Latin American poem, he argues, like Drèze and Sen in relation to child malnutrition in India, that the destruction of the lives of indigenous peoples in the Amazon region is linked to them having no voice in parliament, unlike that of the voices of agribusinesses and timber merchants:

> Many are the trees where torture dwelt, and vast are the forests purchased with a thousand deaths. The timber merchants have members of parliament, while our Amazonia has no one to defend her. . . . They exiled the parrots and the monkeys . . . the chestnut harvests will never be the same.
>
> (QA 9)

For both Sen and the Catholic social tradition, this process of listening, of encounters with the lives of those who have been marginalized, excluded or dispossessed, of enabling their voices to be heard, is transformative for all parties at both the personal and the structural level. Sen talked of the need to bring critical scrutiny to our values and what we hold important in the light of what happens to the lives of others, including distant others (Sen 2002). The Catholic social tradition similarly talks of the need for self-examination, but it also emphasizes the need for acknowledging the harm that has been done to others and ecosystems, through our actions, or lack of actions, and how we could have acted otherwise (LS 218), as a first step towards change. More than Sen's approach to development, which talked in vague terms of the need for value change (from indifference, to attentiveness to the suffering of others, and to solidarity), the Catholic social tradition emphasizes cultural change as a transformational pathway, or what it calls a 'change of heart' (LS 218), a 'bold cultural revolution' (LS 114), a 'profound interior conversion' (LS 217), or an 'ecological conversion' (LS 219) – that is, a change of one's way of relating towards the earth and other people, from domination to care, from indifference to love (LS 217–219).

As Chapter 1 discussed, it also brings to the fore, more than in Sen, the close relationship between transformation of institutions and the transformation of individuals within those institutions, for

> [i]f the laws are to bring about significant, long-lasting effects, the majority of the members of society must be adequately motivated to accept them, and personally transformed to respond. Only by cultivating sound virtues will people be able to make a selfless ecological commitment.
>
> (LS 211)[25]

That economic and political institutions continue to operate in environmentally and socially harmful ways signals, on the one hand, that the people who sustain or support them have not changed their attitudes from lords and masters to carers of nature (QA 56) and, on the other, that the legal structures and macro incentives in which they operate continue to put concerns for short-term economic gains above ecological ones. This is why *Laudato Si'* concludes that what is needed are both 'profound changes in lifestyles, models of production and consumption', and profound changes in 'the established structures of power which today govern societies' (LS 5).[26]

The Catholic social tradition neither specifies how to challenge these established structures of power nor presents particular models of production and consumption. Like Sen's, it leaves it to public reasoning processes in each context and situation to discern what course of action to take in given circumstances, emphasizing that the voices of those who are marginalized be heard in decision-making and emphasizing the need for self-critical examination – that is, critical reflection on the way we live, how we vote, how we produce and consume, how we invest money, and how we work (QA 70).

Concluding remarks

One cannot conclude this chapter without looking at the Catholic Church itself and the lives of its members. The credibility of the Catholic Church's social tradition depends on the way its members live and on how the institutions they create function, whether these are parish communities, religious orders, diocesan structures, non-governmental organizations, or others. As John Paul II already foresaw in 1991, 'Today more than ever, the Church is aware that her social message will gain credibility more immediately from the witness of actions than as a result of its internal logic and consistency' (CA57). The sexual abuse of minors, the covering up of perpetrators, the inaction to protect their victims by those in authority, the abuse of women,[27] the lack of horizontal accountability in clergy being accountable to their bishops and not to the people they serve, the lack of external oversight of finances and transparency in the way money is used and decisions are made, and so forth are all shortcomings of the institutions of the Church themselves in embodying that love and justice that it proclaims.

It is not the task of this book to evaluate the Catholic Church and its institutions in the light of its own social tradition. But let us recall the words of the Second Vatican Council (1964) that the 'Church, embracing in its bosom sinners, at the same time holy and always in need of being purified, always follows the way of penance and renewal' (*Lumen Gentium*, 8), and that Pope Francis is attempting to set the Church on a path to renewal, on a journey of conversion – the subtitle of the 2019 October Synod on the

Amazon was 'New Paths for the Church for an Integral Ecology'. It is plain that Sen's account of public reasoning and listening as governance could give some insights in this process of renewal.

A first insight is that the Catholic social tradition itself can be understood as an outcome of public reasoning processes, and of the lives of individuals and communities and how they respond to the realities they encounter in the light of their faith. The first reflection on the theory and practice of development, the encyclical *Populorum Progressio* by Paul VI, published shortly after development became an international project at the end of colonization period, was the result of the experience of development by local communities. This was discussed and conceptualized by a handful of theologians and social scientists, and this in turn led to a rejection of development as economic growth. Fifty years later, a renewed reflection on development took place on the basis of the realities of communities globally and how they were experiencing social and environmental degradation, and on the basis of scientific research on climate change. The encyclical *Laudato Si'* was the outcome of deliberations with scientists and theologians. This public reasoning process underlying the Catholic social tradition continues to lack transparency, however. The consultants involved in the drafting of encyclicals are not named – although some do talk about their involvement in private circles after an encyclical is released. The Amazon Synod was in that sense breaking new ground with the list of participants clearly presented, as well as the names of those in charge of drafting the final document on the basis of the discussions.[28] More public reasoning and vigorous discussions involving different viewpoints and inclusive of many voices, especially the communities which live in conditions of marginalization and poverty, need to take place. This is probably a reason why Pope Francis insists that his post-apostolic exhortation on the synod, *Querida Amazonia*, does not replace the final document and that both have to be read in conjunction (QA 1–3).

A second insight of Sen's account of public reasoning, and of its furthering by Drydyk (2020a, 2020b), is that public reasoning involves a judgement on how power is held to account and whether decisions can be justified on the basis of their impact on the lives of the most vulnerable and marginalized. Critical reflection on how authority and power are exercised in the institutions of the Church is however a delicate subject, to say the least.

A third insight is that the under-theorizing of power relations in Sen's public reasoning is an invitation to draw on empirical research on the subject. How economic and social inequality is disrupting the democratic process and silencing the voices of the marginalized has been well documented in the social sciences,[29] and Drèze and Sen have discussed the matter at length in their work on India. It could be a new research area for social scientists and theologians to explore power relations within the institutions of the Catholic Church and to bring to light decision-making processes and their effects on the lives of the most vulnerable. There is, to date, very little research on the matter. In that regard, the Catholic social tradition could learn from the processes and analysis of the *Human Development Reports*, with which this book concludes.

Notes

1 See the definition of development research by the UK Development Studies Association as interdisciplinary research which 'concerns the global challenge of combatting poverty, injustice, and environmental degradation', at www.devs tud.org.uk/about/what-is-development-studies/, accessed 13 January 2021.
2 For critical discussions of Sen's *Idea of Justice*, see, among others, Brown (2010), Gotoh and Dumouchel (2009), Meshelski (2019), Osmani (2010), and Robeyns (2012).
3 For Sen's work on famine and hunger, see, among others, Sen (1981), Devereux (2001), De Waal (2004), Drèze and Sen (1989). All the works on Sen and Drèze on hunger in India have now been published as open access by the World Institute for Development Economics Research (Drèze and Sen 2020).
4 The Act was passed in 2005, and anyone can apply to demand access to government documents and information. The government is legally obliged to give them within 30 days (Drèze and Sen 2013: 100).
5 For a discussion on the critical role of listening in democratic decision-making, see Dobson (2014).
6 In 2019, Global Witness (2020) reported 212 killings worldwide for defending their land and homes, half of them in Colombia and the Philippines.
7 Question-and-answer session, launch of *Collective Choice and Social Welfare*, Magdalen College, Oxford, 17 June 2017.
8 For a critical examination of how social media can undermine democracy and public reasoning, see Tucker et al. (2017), Persily and Tucker (2020), Vaidhyanathan (2018).
9 'A reasoned solution of the problem of hunger in the modern world has to acknowledge the importance of well-functioning markets, without denying other forms of participation – through political and democratic process, through public action and influencing state policies, and through cooperation between individuals and social institutions of different types' (Sen 2019: 354).
10 See, for example, Li (2014, 2017, 2018) on the impact of global capitalism and palm oil cultivation on the lives of small farmers in Indonesia.
11 See also Boni and Walker (2013), Walker (2013, 2020).
12 See also Pope Francis's *Querida Amazonia* on the language of love, contemplation and poetry to address our contemporary socio-ecological challenges.
13 Paragraph 70, Final Document of Amazon Synod, www.synod.va/content/ sinodoamazonico/en/documents/final-document-of-the-amazon-synod.html, accessed 13 January 2021.
14 For the relation between love and justice, see also John Paul II's encyclical *Centesimus Annus* issued in 1991: 'Love for others, and in the first place love

for the poor, in whom the Church sees Christ himself, is made concrete in the promotion of justice' (CA58).

15 See also Van Stichel (2014) for a discussion on the creative tension between love and justice in Paul Ricoeur and its implications for the ethics of care.

16 Pope Francis quoted these words of Dom Helder Camara at the end of his Christmas address to the Roman Curia in December 2020; see a video at www. vaticannews.va/en/pope/news/2020-12/pope-francis-curia-christmas-message-crisis-conflict.html, accessed 13 January 2021. They seem to have been omitted in the written version at www.vatican.va/content/francesco/en/speeches/2020/december/documents/papa-francesco_20201221_curia-romana.html, accessed 13 January 2021.

17 For an introduction to liberation theology and its contestation, see, among others, Kirwan (2012), Rowland (2007), Townsend (2018). For the relationship between development and liberation, see, among others, Cooper (2007, 2020). For the influence of liberation theology, and the 'theology of the people' on Pope Francis, see Lakeland (2017), Luciani (2016), Scannone (2016), Shadle (2018: chapters 8–9).

18 See, for example, Ramírez (2016) who discusses that, despite public health access in Mexico through conditional cash transfers programmes, poor women continue to suffer discrimination, abuse, and humiliation in their use of health services because of their treatment by front-line health officers.

19 See their website in Spanish (Encuentro Mundial de Movimientos Populares) at https://movpop.org. The wording of 'popular movements' is a translation from the Spanish 'movimientos populares', which in Argentinian Spanish means movements of the people who live in situations of marginalization and exclusion. Grassroots movements would be a better English translation.

20 See the summary of the meeting at https://movpop.org/2020/10/los-movimien tos-populares-profundizan-en-los-caminos-de-fraternidad-y-dignidad-que-permitan-alcanzar-justicia-social-para-todos, accessed 13 January 2021.

21 www.vatican.va/content/francesco/en/speeches/2015/july/documents/papa-francesco_20150709_bolivia-movimenti-popolari.html, accessed 21 January 2021. For the emphasis on the poor being agents fo their own destiny, see also *Fratelli Tutti* (paragraphs 116 and 169), *Querida Amazonia* (paragraphs 26–27), and Shadle (2018: 288–90). Pope Francis reinforced the importance of agency and accompaniment in his address to young people gathered for the Economy of Francesco event in Assisis in November 2020: '[T]he time has come to take up the challenge of promoting and encouraging models of development, progress and sustainability in which people, especially the excluded (including our sister earth), will no longer be – at most – a merely nominal, technical or functional presence. Instead, they will become protagonists in their own lives and in the entire fabric of society. . . . Let us not think for them, but with them.' See www.vatican.va/content/francesco/en/messages/pont-mes sages/2020/documents/papa-francesco_20201121_videomessaggio-economy-of-francesco.html, accessed 13 January 2021.

22 See Cooper (2020), Farmer (2011), Kerry et al. (2014), Myers (2011) for further discussions on accompaniment.

23 The original quote comes from Archbishop Romero's pastoral letter 'The Church's mission amid the national crisis', 6th August 1979. See www.romerotrust.org.uk/sites/default/files/fourth%20pastoral%20letter.pdf, accessed 13 January 2021.

24 For those who have been assassinated for accompanying people who were being dispossessed of their land in Latin America, see https://redamazonica.org/tag/martires, accessed 13 January 2021.
25 For discussions on the formation of ecological virtues, see, among others, Deane-Drummond (2004, 2008), Northcott (2012), Kureethadam (2016). Kureethadam identifies the following ecological virtues in *Laudato Si'*: praise, gratitude, care, justice, work, sobriety, and humility. For a discussion on ecological virtues within political theory and ecological citizenship, see Dobson (2003).
26 The original quote is from John Paul II, *Centesimus Annus*, paragraph 58.
27 Reports on the extent of abuse have focused on abuse of minors and have been conducted at a diocesan or national level, such as the investigation in Pennsylvania or the Boston dioceses in the United States. There is no report of the extent of abuse globally. As for adult women, some female religious orders have conducted their own reports; see www.nytimes.com/2019/02/06/world/europe/pope-francis-sexual-abuse-nuns.html, accessed 13 January 2021.
28 See www.synod.va/content/sinodoamazonico/en/synod-for-the-amazon.html, accessed 13 January 2021.
29 For a discussion on the social, economic, and political consequences of inequality, see Sánchez-Ancochea (2020).

References

Alkire, Sabina. 2006. "Structural Injustice and Democratic Practice: The Trajectory in Sen's Writings," in Séverine Deneulin, Nicholas Sagovsky and Mathias Nebel (eds), *Transforming Unjust Structures*, Dordrecht: Springer, pp. 47–61.

Azcuy, Virginia and José Juan Cervantes. 2014. "Plaza Pública," in Virginia Azcuy (ed), *Ciudad Vivida. Prácticas de Espiritualidad en Buenos Aires*, Buenos Aires: Editorial Guadalupe, pp. 35–71.

Bebbington, Denise et al. 2019. *Extractive Industry and Infrastructure in the Amazon*, www.climateandlandusealliance.org/reports/impacts-of-extractive-industry-and-infrastructure-on-forests/.

Boni, Alejandra and Melanie Walker (eds). 2013. *Human Development and Capabilities: Re-Imagining the University of the Twenty-First century*, Abingdon: Routledge.

Brown, Chris. 2010. "On Amartya Sen and The Idea of Justice," *Ethics & International Affairs* 24(3): 309–18, doi:10.1111/j.1747-7093.2010.00269.x.

CELAM (Conferencia del Episcopado Latinoamericano y del Caribe). 2007. *Documento Conclusivo de Aparecida*, www.celam.org/aparecida/Espanol.pdf.

Clark, Meghan J. 2020. "Charity, Justice, and Development in Practice: A Case Study of the Daughters of Charity in East Africa," *Journal of Moral Theology* 9(2): 1–14, https://jmt.scholasticahq.com/article/13334-charity-justice-and-development-in-practice-a-case-study-of-the-daughters-of-charity-in-east-africa.

Cooper, Thia. 2007. *Controversies in Political Theology: Development or Liberation?* London: SCM Press.

———. 2020. *A Theology of International Development*, London: Routledge.

Correia, Joel. 2019. "Soy States: Resource Politics, Violent Environments and Soybean Territorialization in Paraguay," *The Journal of Peasant Studies* 46(2): 316–36, https://doi.org/10.1080/03066150.2017.1384726.

Deane-Drummond, Celia E. 2004. *The Ethics of Nature*, Oxford: Blackwell.

———. 2008. "Theology, Ecology, and Values," in Philip Clayton (ed), *The Oxford Handbook of Religion and Science*, doi: 10.1093/oxfordhb/978019 9543656.003.0053.

Devereux, Stephen. 2001. "Sen's Entitlement Approach: Critiques and Counter-Critiques," *Oxford Journal of Development Studies* 29: 245–63.

De Waal, Alex. 2004. *Famine that Kills*, 3rd edition, Oxford: Clarendon Press.

Dobson, Andrew. 2003. *Citizenship and the Environment*, Oxford: Oxford University Press.

———. 2014. *Listening for Democracy: Recognition, Representation, Reconciliation*, Oxford: Oxford University Press.

Drèze, Jean and Amartya Sen. 1989. *Hunger and Public Action*, Oxford: Clarendon Press.

———. 1995. *India: Economic Development and Social Opportunity*, Oxford: Clarendon Press.

———. 2002. *India: Development and Participation*, Oxford: Oxford University Press.

———. 2013. *An Uncertain Glory: India and its Contradictions*, London: Allen Lane.

———. 2020. *Political Economy of Hunger: Volumes 1, 2 and 3*, Oxford: Oxford University Press and Open Access, www.wider.unu.edu/publication/political-economy-hunger-1.

Drydyk, Jay. 2020a. "Capabilities, Public Reason and Democratic Deliberation," in Enrica Chiappero-Martinetti, Siddiq Osmani and Mozaffar Qizilbash (eds), *The Cambridge Handbook of the Capability Approach*, Cambridge: Cambridge University Press, pp. 662–78, https://doi.org/10.1017/9781316335741.037.

———. 2020b. "Democracies Behaving Undemocratically," Unpublished Paper Given at a Panel at a Conference 'Towards an Argentina at the Service of Integral Human Development', 25 November 2020 (recorded talk starting at 55 min on www.youtube.com/watch?v=6HGrc8u3WJk).

Farmer, Paul. 2011. "Accompaniment as Policy," Talk Delivered at the Kennedy School of Government, Harvard University, 25 May 2011, www.lessonsfrom haiti.org/press-and-media/transcripts/accompaniment-as-policy/.

Global Witness. 2020. *Defending Tomorrow*, www.globalwitness.org/en/campaigns/environmental-activists/defending-tomorrow/ (Accessed 13 January 2021).

Gotoh, Reiko and Paul Dumouchel (eds). 2009. *Against Injustice: The New Economics of Amartya Sen*, New York: Cambridge University Press.

Graw Leary, Mary. 2018. "Religious Organizations as Partners in the Global and Local Fight Against Human Trafficking," *The Review of Faith & International Affairs* 16(1): 51–60, doi: 10.1080/15570274.2018.1433583.

Grey, Carmody. 2020. "Time and Measures of Success: Interpreting and Implementing Laudato Si'," *New Blackfriars* 101(1091): 5–28, https://doi.org/10.1111/nbfr.12498.

Hamilton, Lawrence. 2019. *Amartya Sen*, Cambridge: Polity Press.

Ivereigh, Austen. 2010. *Faithful Citizens: A Practical Guide to Catholic Social Teaching and Community Organising*, London: Darton, Longman and Todd.

Kerry, Vanessa et al. 2014. "From Aid to Accompaniment: Rules of the Road for Development Assistance," in Garrett W. Brown, Gavin Yamey and Sarah Wamala (eds), *Handbook of Global Health Policy*, Oxford: Wiley-Blackwell, pp. 483–504.

Khan, Abrahim H. 2012. "Postulating an Affinity: Amartya Sen on Capability and Tagore," *Annals of Neurosciences* 19(1): 3–7, doi: 10.5214/ans.0972.7531.180402.

Kirwan, Michael. 2012. "Liberation Theology and Catholic Social Teaching," *New Blackfriars* 93(1044): 246–58, www.jstor.org/stable/43251618.

Kureethadam, Joshtrom Isaac. 2016. "Ecological Virtues in Laudato Si'," *Ethics in Progress* 7(1), https://doi.org/10.14746/eip.2016.1.4.

Lakeland, Paul. 2017. "Is Pope Francis a Liberation Theologian," in Duncan Dormor and Elena Harris (eds), *Pope Francis, Evangelii Gaudium and the Renewal of the Church*, New York: Paulist Press, chapter 2.

Li, Tania. 2014. *Land's End: Capitalist Relations on an Indigenous Frontier*, Durham, NC: Duke University Press.

———. 2017. "After Development: Surplus Population and the Politics of Entitlement," *Development and Change* 48: 1247–61, doi: 10.1111/dech.12344.

———. 2018. "After the Land Grab: Infrastructural Violence and the 'Mafia System' in Indonesia's Oil Palm Plantation Zones," *Geoforum* 96: 328–37, https://doi.org/10.1016/j.geoforum.2017.10.012.

Lovejoy, Thomas and Carlos Nobre. 2018. "Amazon Tipping Point," *Science Advances* 4(2): 2340, doi: 10.1126/sciadv.aat2340.

Luciani, Rafael. 2016. "La Opción Teológico-Pastoral del Papa Francisco," *Perspectiva Teológica* 48(1), https://doi.org/10.20911/21768757v48n1p81/2016.

McGrath, Simon. 2018. *Education and Development*, Abingdon: Routledge.

Menon, Jaideep C. et al. 2020. "What was right about Kerala's response to the COVID-19 pandemic?" *British Medical Journal Global Health* 5: e003212, http://dx.doi.org/10.1136/bmjgh-2020-003212.

Meshelski, Kristina. 2019. "Amartya Sen's Nonideal Theory," *Ethics & Global Politics* 12(2): 31–45, doi: 10.1080/16544951.2019.1622398.

Myers, Bryant L. 2011. *Walking with the Poor: Principles and Practices of Transformational Development*, Revised edition, Maryknoll, NY: Orbis Books.

Northcott, Michael S. 2012. "Artificial Persons against Nature: Environmental Governmentality, Economic Corporations, and Ecological Ethics," *Annals of the New York Academy of Sciences* 1249(1): 104–17, doi: 10.1111/j.1749-6632.2011.06294.x.

Osmani, Siddiq. 2010. "Theory of Justice for an Imperfect World: Exploring Amartya Sen's Idea of Justice," *Journal of Human Development and Capabilities* 11(4): 599–607, doi: 10.1080/19452829.2010.520965.

Persily, Nathaniel and Joshua Tucker (eds). 2020. *Social Media and Democracy: The State of the Field, Prospects for Reform*, Cambridge: Cambridge University Press.

Pinto, Lucas. 2015. "The Influence of the Pastoral Land Commission (CPT) in the Constitution of the Landless Rural Workers Movement (MST)," *Revista de Estudios Sociales* 51: 76–88, http://dx.doi.org/10.7440/res51.2015.06.

Pope, Stephen. 2019. "Integral Human Development: From Paternalism to Accompaniment," *Theological Studies* 80(1): 123–47, https://doi.org/10.1177/0040563918819798.

Ramírez, Viviana. 2016. "CCTs through a Wellbeing Lens: The Importance of the Relationship between Front-Line Officers and Participants in the Oportunidades/Prospera Programme in Mexico," *Social Policy and Society* 15(3): 451–64, https://doi.org/10.1017/S1474746416000129.

Ricoeur, Paul. 1995. "Love and Justice," *Philosophy & Social Criticism* 21(5–6): 23–39, https://doi.org/10.1177/0191453795021005-604.

———. 2000. *The Just* (trans, D. Pellauer), Chicago: University of Chicago Press.

Ritchie, Angus. 2019. *Inclusive Populism: Creating Citizens in the Global Age*, Notre Dame, Indiana: University of Notre Dame Press.

Robeyns, Ingrid. 2012. "Are Transcendental Theories of Justice Redundant?" *Journal of Economic Methodology* 19(2): 159–64, doi: 10.1080/1350178X.2012.683587.

Rowland, Christopher (ed). 2007. *The Cambridge Companion to Liberation Theology*, 2nd edition. Cambridge: Cambridge University Press.

Sánchez-Ancochea, Diego. 2020. *The Costs of Inequality in Latin America: Lessons and Warnings for the Rest of the World*. London: IB Tauris.

Scannone, Juan Carlos. 2016. "Pope Francis and the Theology of the People," *Theological Studies* 77(1): 118–35, doi: 10.1177/0040563915621141.

Second Vatican Council. 1964. *Lumen Gentium: Dogmatic Constitution of the Church*, www.vatican.va/archive/hist_councils/ii_vatican_council/documents/vat-ii_const_19641121_lumen-gentium_en.html.

Sen, Amartya. 1981. *Poverty and Famines: An Essay on Entitlement and Deprivation*, Oxford: Clarendon Press.

———. 1993. "Markets and Freedoms: Achievements and Limitations of the Market Mechanism in Promoting Individual Freedoms," *Oxford Economic Papers* 45(4): 519–54.

———. 1999. *Development as Freedom*, Oxford: Oxford University Press.

———. 2002. "Open and Closed Impartiality," *The Journal of Philosophy* 99(9): 445–69, https://doi.org/10.2307/3655683.

———. 2006. *The Argumentative Indian: Writings on Indian History, Culture and Identity*, London: Penguin.

———. 2009. *The Idea of Justice*, London: Allen Lane.

———. 2015. "Universal Healthcare: The Affordable Dream," *The Guardian*, 6 January 2015, www.theguardian.com/society/2015/jan/06/-sp-universal-healthcare-the-affordable-dream-amartya-sen.

———. 2019. "The Political Economy of Hunger: On Reasoning and Participation," *Common Knowledge* 25(1): 348–56, https://muse.jhu.edu/article/727152 (originally published in 1994).

———. 2020a. "Listening as Governance," *Indian Express*, 8 April 2020, https://indianexpress.com/article/opinion/columns/coronavirus-india-lockdown-amartya-sen-economy-migrants-6352132/.

————. 2020b. "A Better Society Can Emerge," *Financial Times*, 15 April, www. ft.com/content/5b41ffc2-7e5e-11ea-b0fb-13524ae1056b.

————. 2020c. "The Future of Development," online lecture given for the Human Development Report Office, 12 November, https://futureofdevelopment.undp. org/content/fod/en/home/our-products/conversing-with-the-mind-that-put-human-in-development.html.

Shadle, Matthew. 2018. *Interrupting Capitalism: Catholic Social Teaching and the Economy*, Oxford: Oxford University Press.

Tilky, Leon. 2020. *Education for Sustainable Development in the Postcolonial World*, Abingdon: Routledge.

Townsend, Nick. 2018. "The Challenges of Liberation Theology and Neoconservative Capitalism," in *Virtual Plater: Catholic Social Teaching Gateway*, Newman University College, Module B, Unit 6, https://virtualplater.org.uk/ (Accessed 3 December 2020).

Tucker, Joshua et al. 2017. "From Liberation to Turmoil: Social Media and Democracy," *Journal of Democracy* 28(4): 46–59, doi: 10.1353/jod.2017.0064.

Vaidhyanathan, Siva. 2018. *Anti-Social Media: How Facebook Disconnects Us and Undermines Democracy*, New York: Oxford University Press.

Van Stichel, Ellen. 2014. "Love and Justice's Dialectical Relationship: Ricoeur's Contribution on the Relationship between Care and Justice within Care Ethics," *Medicine, Health Care and Philosophy* 17: 499–508, doi: 10.1007/s11019-013-9536-7.

Vaughan, Rosie P. and Melanie Walker. 2012. "Capabilities, Values and Education Policy," *Journal of Human Development and Capabilities* 13(3): 495–512, doi: 10.1080/19452829.2012.679648.

Walker, Melanie. 2013. "Critical Capability Pedagogies and University Education," *Educational Philosophy and Theory* 42(8): 898–917, doi: 10.1111/j.1469-5812.2007.00379.x.

————. 2020. "On Education and Capabilities Expansion," in Enrica Chiappero-Martinetti, Siddiqur Osmani and Mozaffar Qizilbash (eds), *The Cambridge Handbook of the Capability Approach*, pp. 505–522, https://doi.org/10.1017/9781316335741.029.

Walker, Melanie and Merridy Wilson-Strydom. 2016. *Socially Just Pedagogies, Capabilities and Quality in Higher Education: Global Perspectives*, London: Palgrave Macmillan.

Conclusion

In December 2020, the UNDP released its thirtieth anniversary *Human Development Report*, entitled *The Next Frontier: Human Development and the Anthropocene* (referred to in what follows as the *Report*). The *Report* takes the human development framework in new directions which mirror many of this book's arguments. Whether the encyclical *Laudato Si'*, the Pope's visit to the United Nations Environment Programme (UNEP) in Nairobi in November 2015, and his meeting with its then Executive Director, Achim Steiner, and now Administrator of UNDP[1] had an influence on the *Report* is difficult to establish. The many alarm bells about the last call for action that have been raised by the Intergovernmental Panel on Climate Change,[2] and by many other institutions and prominent individuals like Sir David Attenborough and Greta Thunberg, and not least the Covid-19 global pandemic, have undoubtedly influenced the radical change of course in the way the *Human Development Reports* have conceived development so far. This concluding chapter critically discusses the *Report* in the light of the arguments laid out in the previous chapters.

Sen's capability approach to development and that of the UNDP reports have been very close from the outset. Under the direction of Mahbub ul-Haq, previous minister of planning in Pakistan, and Sen's long-time friend since their PhD student days at the University of Cambridge, the UNDP launched in 1990 its flagship annual publication.[3] The Human Development Index (HDI), a composite index which integrates life expectancy, years of schooling, and gross domestic product per capita, would become the trademark of the reports. The political success of the HDI would however come to eclipse the richness of the human development lens. Human development is not an index but a conceptual framework to assess how people's lives are doing and to analyse what may hinder or facilitate the conditions under which people can live flourishing lives.[4]

DOI: 10.4324/9781003121534-5

This book has considered human development as the conception of development which can be derived from the freedom perspective, in its dual aspects of well-being and agency that Sen has proposed. It has therefore taken human development and Sen's capability approach to development as synonyms and interchangeable.[5] Its fundamental features include attention to the kinds of lives that people live, concern for the vulnerable and marginalized, and the centrality of agency in transforming situations and creating the conditions for people to live better lives. Another fundamental feature, which this book has often emphasized, is its open-endedness. The *Report* describes human development as a 'journey, not a destination' (UNDP 2020: 6). It views the human development approach as 'permanently under construction' and 'open ended to new and emerging challenges and opportunities' (UNDP 2020: 43). Given the current context of climate emergency, and the global pandemic which has laid bare the deep interconnections between all life systems, the *Report* is framing a new human development narrative, which 'places people's interaction with nature in historical, social, and economic contexts, informed by insights from the natural sciences' (UNDP 2020: 53). This integration of human and earth systems marks a departure from previous reports. The environment is no longer seen as a separate realm, acting as a constraint upon or facilitator of human flourishing. Humans are part of nature and not separate from it. The human development challenge is therefore 'to redress both social and planetary imbalances' (UNDP 2020: 22), to 'expand human freedoms in balance with the planet' (UNDP 2020: 104).

The *Report* both extends the conception of human development to integrate the earth, and maintains a central concern for people's lives, especially the marginalized, and for human agency. The running theme of the *Report* is that we have the choice to continue business as usual, and face catastrophic consequences, or to live differently. It characterizes the Anthropocene as an 'age defined by human choice' (UNDP 2020: iii). If we humans have through our actions modified the earth's crust, so too we can choose to act differently to address current social and planetary imbalances. If the rallying call of Pope Francis in *Laudato Si'* is that it is 'we human beings above all who need to change' (LS 202) to remedy the damage we have done, this is also the rallying call of the 2020 *Human Development Report*. It is we humans who have to choose to do things differently.

One way in which the *Report* has chosen to do things differently is by changing its flagship Human Development Index. It proposes a new experimental index, the Planetary Pressures–adjusted HDI (P-HDI), which adjusts the HDI with a factor that includes measures of per capita carbon dioxide emissions and material footprints (UNDP 2020: 235–6). Its aim is to incentivize change and 'learn from countries which are moving in the right direction' (UNDP 2020: 235). Norway and Iceland, for example, make it into the top five in the HDI ranking but are down 15 and 26 places respectively in the P-HDI ranking. Luxembourg and Singapore are the countries which experience the largest fall in ranking, making them among the least sustainable countries in those terms. Costa Rica improves its ranking significantly when its HDI is adjusted for planetary pressures.[6]

One of the *Report*'s central arguments is that planetary and social imbalances reinforce each other. Imbalances in human systems, such as inequality and lack of voice and representation of those most at risk of climate change, lead to imbalances in earth systems. This then deepens imbalances of human systems with the poor suffering most from planetary imbalances. In sum, one could say that the more than 400 pages of the *Report* elaborate and expand the following two sentences of *Laudato Si'*: 'The human environment and the natural environment deteriorate together; we cannot adequately combat environmental degradation unless we attend to causes related to human and social degradation' (LS 48); 'Today, however, we have to realize that a true ecological approach always becomes a social approach; it must integrate questions of justice in debates on the environment, so as to hear both the cry of the earth and the cry of the poor' (LS 49). One could also say that the *Report* fleshes out the implications of *Laudato Si'*'s argument that 'everything is connected' (LS 16, 70, 91, 117, 220, 240). It takes the interconnectedness among all life systems as a fundamental category. It sees 'social and natural systems as embedded in each other' (UNDP 2020: 23). It contends that 'the human development journey cannot be separated from the web of life we are embedded in' (UNDP 2020: 21). It considers the narrative of the Anthropocene as 'a catalyst for systemic thinking about the interdependence of people and nature' (UNDP 2020: 55). It argues for 'reimagining the human development journey as one in which people are embedded in the biosphere' (UNDP 2020: 223). It takes inspiration in that regard from indigenous peoples in the United States for whom:

> Nature is understood as full of relatives not resources, where inalienable rights are balanced with inalienable responsibilities and where wealth itself is measured not by resources ownership and control, but by the number of good relationships we maintain in the complex and diverse life systems of this blue green planet.
>
> (UNDP 2020: 88)[7]

The *Report* does not make value judgements about whether one should abandon the language of seeing nature as a set of natural resources or whether one should start talking instead of nature as a set of relatives to whom one has obligations. As it says on many occasions, it wants to open up a conversation about how to live differently, how to take different actions, how to make different policy decisions. UNDP Administrator Achim Steiner expresses the aspiration for the *Report* 'to open a new conversation on the path ahead for each country – a path yet unexplored' (UNDP 2020: iii). This is a similar call to that found in *Laudato Si'*, in which Pope Francis 'urgently appeal[s] for a new dialogue about how we are shaping the future of our planet' (LS 11).

References are made to religious traditions, and wisdom traditions more widely, as conversation partners in the public reasoning process on how humans can act differently so as to reestablish the balance between human and earth systems. It mentions the Quranic concept of *tawheed* (oneness), which points to the unity of all creation and past and future generations (UNDP 2020: 88);[8] *Laudato Si'* for a Christian interpretation of this unity of all creation and our embeddedness in nature (UNDP 2020: 88); the Māori notion of *whakapapa*; and the Latin American indigenous notion of 'good living' or living in harmony (UNDP 2020: 90; cf. Chapter 2). The *Report* concludes that 'recognizing our humanity as part of a larger network of connections that include all living things is part of philosophical traditions worldwide' (UNDP 2020: 88).

Another of the central themes of the *Report* is the role of agency. It is a certain way of exercising our human freedom that has led to the current imbalances. As the *Report* puts it, 'Human choices, shaped by values and institutions, have given rise to the interconnected planetary and social imbalances we face' (UNDP 2020: 5). The *Report* makes several references to Sen's argument that '[t]he reach of reasoned and interactive agency . . . can be particularly crucial for our transition to sustainability' (Sen 2013: 18).[9] It discusses the role of public reasoning, agency, and collective action in changing a society's values around nature and social norms about what is acceptable or non-acceptable behaviour – for example, flying to a destination when less carbon-intensive means of transport are available. There is however a departure from previous reports on the centrality of freedom and agency. The exercise of human freedom is this time oriented towards what the Catholic social tradition would call the common good, which the *Report* understands as a restored balance between human and earth systems, or the promotion of flourishing of both each person and ecosystems. The *Report* asks, 'How can we use our power to expand human freedoms while easing planetary pressures'? (UNDP 2020: 70). Humans can choose to act and transform their societies to make them carbon neutral and with zero waste while attending to the most marginalized, or they can choose to do nothing or little. Perhaps the *Report* could have mentioned in that regard Sen's distinction between an optimal and maximal decision. It may not be possible to decide whether it is better to reduce carbon emissions through 'having a carbon-pricing through a market mechanism' (alternative x) or through 'regulating and banning of certain carbon activities' (alternative y) (Sen 2017a: 461). One should bear in mind that alternative z, doing nothing, is worse than alternative x or y (Sen 2017a, 2017b).[10] Sen (2017a: 458) concludes that instead of continuing the search for ranking 'x' against 'y', leaving the pair unranked, and making a choice despite no best solution and despite difference of views, is not unreasonable; it 'may even be a common outcome of reasoned analysis of ethical and political evaluation' (Sen 2017a: 458).

As in the Catholic social tradition, the 2020 *Human Development Report* also integrates the self as a subject of development (cf. Chapter 1). Its emphasis on human agency applies at both the individual and the collective level. We have to make choices, as individuals and as groups (in terms of transport, diet, modes of consumption and production, etc.), and become stewards of nature (UNDP 2020: 88–93). In its rethinking of human development, it argues for paying attention to the 'value of people's inner lives' (UNDP 2020: 112)[11] and also 'for the need to rethink "human," our humanity' (UNDP 2020: 112). What are the conditions that make us human has become a key question for development research, as the Catholic social tradition had long argued (cf. Chapter 2). The co-construction of human and non-human natures in different cultures needs to become an essential area of inquiry (UNDP 2020: 112).

As in previous years, the *Report* emphasizes the importance of analysing and changing power relations, but it does so with much more prominence. Its underlying message is that human and life systems will not be brought back into balance without a radical transformation of power relations, and without addressing socio-economic and political inequalities, for 'nature's [and human] degradation is often linked with power imbalances' (UNDP 2020: 72). This is why the *Report* urges us 'to seriously attend to the structural conditions and violence creating and perpetuating inequalities – and listen to and include the experiences and priorities of those most marginalized' (UNDP 2020: 113). It makes a plea for the voices of those who suffer from environmental and social harms to be better represented in policy decision-making processes. Like Pope Francis who, citing a Latin American poem, lamented that 'The timber merchants have members of parliament, while our Amazonia has no one to defend her' (QA 9), so does the *Report* lament that 'Many vulnerable communities lack the financial resources and organizational clout to sustain a long-term fight when there is a threat to their well-being. And they have fewer advocates and lobbyists pushing for their interests at the national level' (UNDP 2020: 67). When they try to speak out and defend their lives, 'they are limited . . . by asymmetries in power that muffle their voices' (UNDP 2020: 68).

Given the similarities between the Catholic social tradition and the reimagined human development perspectives of the 2020 *Human Development Report*, one could wonder whether bringing them into dialogue has now become redundant. There are however some significant mutually beneficial contributions that both can continue to offer. The contributions from the human development approach that this book has highlighted are a greater engagement with a gender perspective and a richer empirical social and political analysis. These could be included much more in further developments of the Catholic social tradition. The *Report* offers many examples of analysing social realities taking into account the differentiated impact of climate change on women, and especially women who live in situations of vulnerability. It also provides more detailed analysis of how power relations, and the lack of voice and representation of marginalized communities, affect people's lives and increase ecological pressures.

This book has highlighted that opening up to the spiritual dimension in development entails being open to the values of love and friendship, of gift, of transcendence. In some ways, the reimagined human development perspective of the *Report* does the same by referring to indigenous and religious traditions that see nature as a gift that is bequeathed to future generations and with whom humans are in mutual relationships. But it does not develop this much – for example, on how love can provide the foundation of solidarity and the motivation from which to make choices that bring human and planetary systems back into balance with each other. For the Catholic social tradition, development is not complete without love (cf. Chapter 1). This focus on love can provide the motivation for choosing differently, for living differently, for making different policy choices, and also for accepting some of the sacrifices or inconveniences which may go with it. Love leads to attentiveness, to listening to the silenced vulnerable and suffering person and to the earth (cf. Chapter 2). It starts a process of journeying together, whatever our levels of privilege and vulnerability, on a path of mutual transformation (cf. Chapter 3). Through its presence among both vulnerable and more privileged communities, the Catholic Church could play a more significant role in building networks of global solidarity and in being a channel through which those voices silenced by power relations could be amplified. The Amazon Synod in October 2019 was a step in that direction, in providing a discussion platform where vulnerable communities could express what ails their lives and be strengthened in their representative organizations.

The Catholic social tradition put forward the concept of integral human development in the late 1960s to articulate its perspective on international development. In 2015, it put forward the concept of integral ecology, while continuing to use the former. The two could be seen as synonyms, with the former more common in the development studies/social sciences field and the latter in the environmental studies/natural sciences field.[12] The UN has translated the development perspective that Amartya Sen has as 'human development'. In 2020, it has continued to use the terminology of 'human development' to articulate its perspective on international development, albeit radically rethinking its meaning by moving it in the direction of integral human development/integral ecology. These so-called secular and faith-based perspectives are moving in the same direction. Whatever the name given – human development, integral human development, or integral ecology – there is only one way forward for humanity: to rethink what it means to be human and become more aware of our common belonging in a common home, together with other human beings as well as animals, plants, rivers, air, soil, glaciers, and other components of earth systems. The challenge remains of how the analytical lenses of human development (in its renewed 2020 vision) and integral human development/integral ecology could combine forces to become mobilizing frames for all actors at all levels of society. Were they to do so, they could enable households, educational bodies, churches, mosques, municipal governments, and business organizations, among other kinds of institutions, to embark on the journey of transformation to bring all life systems, human and non-human, back into balance.

Notes

1 https://news.un.org/en/story/2015/11/516592-pope-francis-calls-strong-climate-agreement-during-visit-un-office-nairobi, accessed 19 January 2021.
2 In October 2018, the IPPC estimated that there was only a 12-year window to take action to avoid catastrophic climate change; see https://news.un.org/en/story/2018/10/1022492, accessed 19 January 2021.
3 See Amartya Sen's special contribution on 'Human Development and Mahbub-ul Haq' and how their friendship shaped the *Report* (UNDP 2020: xi). See also Gasper (2011).
4 See, among others, Fukuda-Parr and Kumar (2009), Prabhu and Iyer (2019), Stewart, Ranis and Samman (2018).
5 In her account of the capability approach, Robeyns (2017: 197–202) contends that the two need to be carefully distinguished. She justifies the distinction on the grounds that (1) human development has wider intellectual roots; (2) the capability approach is used for a wide range of purposes beyond mere development concerns; (3) the human development approach implicitly conveys a developing/developed country dichotomy, which the capability approach seeks to supersede; (4) human development is presented as an alternative policy paradigm to neo-liberalism, whilst the capability approach is simply an evaluative framework. This book has however not been concerned with the 'capability approach' in the abstract but as a specific approach for thinking about development.

6 See UNDP (2020: 241–4) for the comparative table of all countries of their HDI and P-HDI.
7 The original quote is from Wildcat (2013: 515).
8 For an Islamic perspective on development and care for the earth, see Khan and Cheema (2020).
9 See also Sen (2017a: 40) for the role of public reasoning in value change with regard to the environment.
10 Sen (2017a: xxix) defines an optimal alternative as one 'that is at least as good as every other alternative' and maximal as one 'which is not worse than any other alternative'. In this case, the decisions to introduce carbon-pricing or regulations are both maximal decisions, as one cannot rank them against each other.
11 For a discussion of the neglect of people's inner worlds in development, see Ives, Freeth and Fischer (2020).
12 See Deane-Drummond and Deneulin (2020) for a discussion on integral human development and integral ecology and their differences of emphasis.

References

Deane-Drummond, Celia and Séverine Deneulin. 2020. *Integral Ecology: A Concept Note for Policy and Practice*, Laudato Si' Research Institute, Campion Hall: University of Oxford, https://lsri.campion.ox.ac.uk/.

Fukuda-Parr, Sakiko and A. K. Shiva Kumar (eds). 2009. *Handbook of Human Development: Concepts, Measures, and Policies*, New Delhi: Oxford University Press.

Gasper, Des. 2011. "Pioneering the Human Development Revolution: Analysing the Trajectory of Mahbub ul Haq," *Journal of Human Development and Capabilities* 12(3): 433–56, doi: 10.1080/19452829.2011.576660.

Ives, Christopher D., Rebecca Freeth and Joern Fischer. 2020. "Inside-Out Sustainability: The Neglect of Inner Worlds," *Ambio* 49: 208–17, https://doi.org/10.1007/s13280-019-01187-w.

Khan, Ajaz Ahmed and Affan Cheema. 2020. *Islam and International Development: Insights for Working with Muslim Communities*, Rugby: Practical Action Publishing.

Prabhu, Seeta and Sandhya Iyer. 2019. *Human Development in an Unequal World*, New Delhi: Oxford University Press.

Robeyns, Ingrid. 2017. *Wellbeing, Freedom and Social Justice: The Capability Approach Re-Examined*, Cambridge: Open Book Publishers, www.openbookpublishers.com/product/682.

Sen, Amartya. 2013. "The Ends and Means of Sustainability," *Journal of Human Development and Capabilities* 14(1): 6–20, doi: 10.1080/19452829.2012.747492.

———. 2017a. *Collective Choice and Social Welfare*, London: Allen Lane.

———. 2017b. "Reason and Justice: The Optimal and the Maximal," *Philosophy* 92(1): 5–19, https://doi.org/10.1017/S0031819116000309.

Stewart, Frances, Gustav Ranis and Emma Samman. 2018. *Advancing Human Development: Theory and Practice*, Oxford: Oxford University Press.

United Nations Development Programme (UNDP). 2020. *Human Development Report. The Next Frontier: Human Development and the Anthropocene*, http://hdr.undp.org/.

Wildcat, Daniel R. 2013. "Introduction: Climate Change and Indigenous Peoples of the USA," *Climatic Change* 120: 509–15, doi: 10.1007/s10584-013-0849-6.

Index

Printed in the United States
by Baker & Taylor Publisher Services

.